Vintage Fashion and Couture

Vintage Fashion and Couture

From Poiret to McQueen

Kerry Taylor

Foreword by Hubert de Givenchy **Prologue** by Christopher Kane

FIREFLY BOOKS

CONTENTS

HUBERT DE GIVENCHY

I would like to thank Kerry Taylor for her crucial work researching the most important fashion collections – and more particularly haute couture – and for her evaluation of key periods when creators designed magnificent costumes that are now much sought after on account of their rarity. The appeal of couture is ever increasing, as witnessed by the growth of what is today called "vintage".

This book shows Kerry Taylor's marvellous research on quality clothing. I would, therefore, like to evoke in these few lines her great talent and enthusiasm, which I admire as much as for her insightful comments on Givenchy.

Hubert de Givenchy

Dior began the design process with a pencil sketch. Givenchy and Madame Grès preferred to start with a great fabric. Vionnet liked to drape fabric onto a miniature mannequin and the toiles were then taken from that. How do you begin the design process?

With each new project my starting point is drawing; it always has been. I can't begin to think of colours, textures, and fabrics until I have sketches that inspire me, which can be very problematic when dealing with multiple suppliers and manufacturers who have strict deadlines. What really works for me is to sketch in front of the TV. People laugh but it makes me feel relaxed.

Schiaparelli had a design theme such as the circus. Are you a bit like Schiap? Your previous collections' themes have included electric brain pulses and Frankenstein. Where do the ideas spring from?

You will never believe this but the themes that occur in my work arrive in the latter stages of the overall creation of the collection. It is a bit hit and miss; there is no formula or science to it. Each season is very different but somehow everything comes together near the end… And then I will be reminded of something from my childhood or a character from a film.

In the old couture houses in the 1950s they had two shows a year, each one with up to 200 models, all of which had its own name. That sounds like a lot, but in the 21st century you have the main ready-to-wear collections in Spring/Summer and Autumn/Winter. In addition, there are resort and pre-collections and there are important fashion weeks in Milan, New York, Paris, and London. This seems like a massive workload for one person. How do you cope?

I suppose I don't know anything else, so I just get on with it. I come from a working-class family with a strong work ethic. I feel very happy when working despite the critical paths and multiple deadlines. I have to say that, when I look back, I don't know how I managed working on Versus as well as my own line. It was a real challenge but the rewards far outweighed the difficulties.

Do you think you will ever produce a couture line…? Would you like to?

I hope so. I find the world of couture fascinating. It's something for the future.

Nothing in fashion is new. Are there elements in your work that might be influenced by vintage? Are there any particular decades you love or that inspire you? For the "Frankenstein" collection, to me there was a very strong futuristic, sixties Courrèges feel about it, for instance. It was probably unintentional, but that's what I felt looking at all the shimmering silver and pastel shades.

I love looking at historical pieces of clothing; they can be so inspiring and lead to new ideas. Personally, I want to work on making collections that are new and innovative; I don't want to repeat what another designer has done. That said, I really love the sixties period for its innovative uses of new materials such as plastics, metals, and so on.

Prologue

CHRISTOPHER KANE

My love of fashion began early – I still possess a 1930s sequined capelet for which I saved up my pocket money. I remember the wonder of the first flapper dress I handled that came into Sotheby's for valuation in 1979, how the sequins caught the light, and the sheer weight of the beadwork. It seemed to capture a lost moment in time. I've handled hundreds of them over the years but I still find them mesmerizing, especially if they carry a couture label hidden down a side seam. I have had the pleasure of handling antique pieces by Charles Frederick Worth right the way through to cutting-edge 21st-century examples by Junya Watanabe and everything in between. I have been privileged to handle fabulous single-owner collections, including the wardrobes of the Duke and Duchess of Windsor, the Honourable Daphne Guinness, Jerry Hall, and Marie Helvin, as well as historically important pieces belonging to Marilyn Monroe, Elizabeth Taylor, and Ava Gardner. But it's the garments themselves, even without these wonderful provenances, that are so special.

I have not been able to include examples by every major designer in this book and I apologize for that in advance. However, I have tried to give an impression of the market as a whole and where possible have used actual examples that I have sold at auction.

What is vintage?

For me, vintage is a garment that possesses age, beauty, and great design. So much that is described as "vintage" is just second-hand clothing and the vintage tag just an excuse for overcharging. "Couture" is another word recklessly bandied about and sometimes incorrectly applied by vintage dealers to designer-labelled ready-to-wear. Haute couture is the highest form of fashion excellence in its design, fabric, and execution (with hand-finished internal seams).

The demise of haute couture in the 21st century

Yves Saint Laurent produced his last couture collection in 2002 and Valentino in 2008.

Today Karl Lagerfeld for Chanel, Raf Simons for Dior, and Jean Paul Gaultier retain their couture lines, but the number of clients willing to pay couture prices is relatively small compared to the 1950s when couture was more affordable and more widely worn. As so little haute couture is now made and the skills so prized for centuries are being eroded and lost, vintage haute couture pieces from the first half of the 20th century, made from the finest fabrics with hand-finishing and adornments, are even more prized. There is a finite supply of early pieces, yet the number of collectors continues to grow. As the rarity of these masterpieces increases year on year, their prices also escalate. Vintage couture can only grow in importance as the early reference pieces of the 20th century become increasingly harder to find.

Who buys vintage?

The market for good vintage fashion has grown rapidly since the early 2000s. There have always been serious collectors who see vintage fashion as an art form and an investment but these are relatively small in number. The market increase is largely due to those who wish to buy to wear. Vintage fashion is good value, generally good quality, and unusual compared to what one finds in retail shops. Kate Moss and Hollywood starlets wearing vintage on the red carpet have also fuelled demand.

Fashion exhibitions attract crowds and raise much-needed museum funds, and major ones can often cause a spike in price for a related designer or period. Fashion houses themselves are eager to acquire examples of their heritage, not only as a record of their history but to add prestige to their brand.

Vintage as a design source

Contemporary designers, sometimes consciously or unconsciously, take inspiration from vintage and reinterpret historic looks. Since the 1990s there hasn't really been a single overriding "look" and recent trends such as hippy boho-chic, eighties power-shoulders,

Introduction

KERRY TAYLOR

and twenties beaded dresses have incorporated vintage elements.

In the 1950s a couturier had just two couture shows per year, albeit with several hundred models in each. In contrast, the modern designer has to cope with two ready-to-wear lines, pre-collections, resort collections, and accessory lines. Some simultaneously design men's as well as women's lines.

This relentless quest for new ideas often leads designers to vintage for inspiration – for a closure, a sleeve shape, or a clever dress construction. A band of couture beading or fragment of embroidery might trigger a new theme or design that is reinterpreted in a fresh, contemporary manner. Occasionally, an entire garment has been copied and the modern designer label added. Thankfully this is the exception rather than the rule.

In pursuit of vintage

Even today I meet clients who have discovered a valuable couture treasure at a car boot sale or a vintage market. This book highlights some of these treasures including the Chanel 1928 printed lace dress that was bought as a bundle in a carrier bag for £150 ($240; page 39) and the Schiaparelli dress that was rescued from a moth-infested trunk.

One of my greatest pleasures is rummaging through a collection of clothes, discovering a label hidden inside a dress, or recognizing a design from an archive photograph or a couture piece from its construction and finish. I have made some of my most incredible discoveries in trunks left forgotten in attics, and today many of these finds are now in museums and important private collections the world over. It gives me great pleasure to see them displayed in all their glory and to know that I played a part in rescuing them.

A note on price estimates

Throughout the book, I have included value codes to give an idea of what different pieces are currently worth. Please consult page 224 for further details.

Above, Christian Dior "Jean-Pierre Grédy" cocktail ensemble, 1952: fuchsia silk chiffon with fichu neckline over black taffeta skirt.

King Edward VII's court ushered in an era of opulence with exquisite, expensive gowns in rich brocades and sweet-pea satins, dripping with embroidery and lace. The fashionable ideal was the curvaceous, well upholstered matron, whose corsets thrust the breasts forward forming a "monobosom" above a tiny waist. Early 20th-century dresses tended to be formed out of separate bodices and skirts, with one-piece princess lines introduced around 1905. Often, all that remains today are the bodices, the skirts having been cannibalized for fabric during the world wars. Dresses bore their maker's name on the waist-stay, the woven petersham waistband that anchored the bodice in place. Leading couturiers around 1900 were from French Maisons Worth, Vionnet, Lanvin, Lucile, Paquin, Doucet, Redfern, Callot, Rouff, Boue Sœurs, Chéruit, Pingat, and Poiret. Finding good examples from the 1900–1910 period is difficult because the tin washes, used to give better weight, caused disintigration. Even if the outer dress is in good condition, the inner lining has usually perished.

The affluent, refined Edwardian lady spent her time changing outfits – a déshabillé robe, followed by a morning dress, an afternoon or slightly smarter reception dress, an orientalist tea gown (like a lavish dressing gown) where her corset could be removed at five o'clock when she would take tea, have a cigarette, and receive friends, and finally a dinner gown (with corset) or opulent ball gown. Day necklines tended to be high with wired collars and bodice waists cut lower at the front than the back, layers of lace-trimmed petticoats, chemises, drawers, silk stockings, and garters. Charles Dana Gibson's American "Gibson Girl" encapsulated the curvaceous look.

Generally, by 1907 the waistline was no longer drawn up higher behind than in front and it began to rise above the natural waist. By 1908 silhouettes became more vertical. Smart, masculine tailored day suits were frequently worn (especially by suffragettes), and hats, often laden with flowers and feathers, grew in width and height. Large muffs, feather boas, fur stoles, and knee-high leather boots were popular. Linen and silk "duster" coats were worn for motoring, accompanied by goggles or visors and large hats tied on with scarves.

Changing tastes

Fashions become more youthful following Edward VII's death (1910), with a natural bust over a slim cylindrical skirt and hemlines so narrow that they were christened "hobble" skirts. Empire and Directoire influences were seen in day- and eveningwear and Poiret tried to persuade women into brassieres and harem trousers. The 1913 tango craze made hobble skirts unpractical and hats grew smaller. With the outbreak of war, waistlines descended and widened, hems became fuller and above ankle length, and evening gowns had draped tiers and long narrow trains. By 1916 the brassiere replaced the corset and camisole and skirts had wide petersham waistbands, often featuring narrow maker's labels. Sailor collars and military touches are often found in wartime clothes, and by 1917 skirts were wider and flared or barrel-shaped as women took on men's jobs. By 1918 the bosom lost definition, as interest shifted to the ankles and legs.

Fabulous gowns and their immediate successors are fairly rare in good condition and still relatively cheap. Unless they bear the label of a major fashion house, they are usually very under priced and under-appreciated.

Below, Worth signature label, part of the waistband of a c.1900 gown.

Right, Coats and cloaks, 1908: engraving from *Les Robes de Paul Poiret* by Paul Iribe.

Introduction

THE TWENTIETH CENTURY BEGINS

"It was equally in the name of Liberty that I proclaimed the fall of the corset and the adoption of the brassiere which, since then, has won the day." *Paul Poiret*

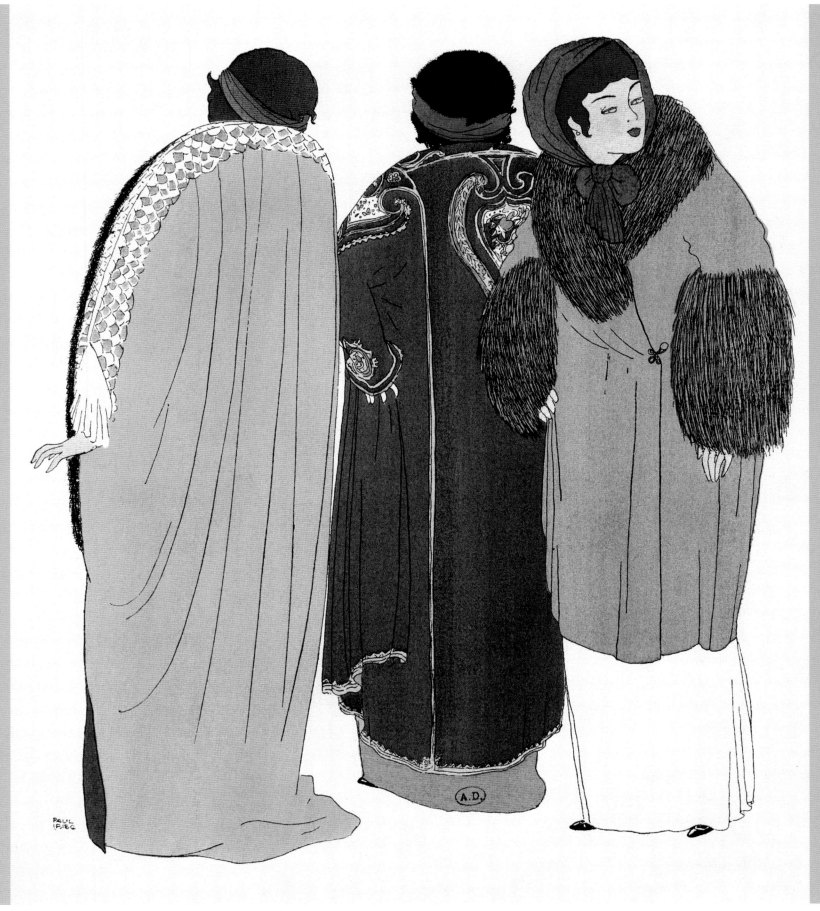

Far left and left, Worth ball gown, *c.*1900: pink damask woven satin with beaded side panels, and sleeves embroidered in metal threads and diamanté studs. L. Printed silk gown, attributed to Poiret, *c.*1912: grey crêpe de Chine, the skirt front held in a drape that falls to points at the sides, culminating in grey silk tassels. M

Below, Madame Ernest Ltd cinnamon gauze silk and satin evening gown with hobble skirt, *c.*1910. L

Right, Camille Clifford – the original "Gibson Girl", 1905. In the early twentieth century the hourglass figure and towering coiffure defined the ideal of feminine beauty.

The larger-than-life French couturier Paul Poiret (1879–1944) worked for Jacques Doucet and Maison Worth before setting up his own establishment in 1903 where his clientele included Lillie Langtry, Sarah Bernhardt, Isadora Duncan, and Nancy Cunard.

Poiret is credited with freeing women from corsets, advocating a more natural, un-corseted (though sometimes lightly boned) line. Poiret produced delightful columnar dresses of crisp white organdie with accents of brilliant colour, such as hot pink stripes or edgings, or pretty oriental embroidered details. These romantic neoclassical fashions were reproduced in high-quality pochoir prints by Georges Lepape and Paul Iribe in specially commissioned books – *Les Choses de Paul Poiret* (1911), *Les Robes de Paul Poiret* (1908) – and in the fashion periodical *La Gazette du Bon Ton* (1912–25), which are all highly desirable in their own right.

International influences

In contrast to the prevailing S-shape silhouette, Poiret's dresses have a pared-down elegance. Many early creations were based on simply cut, rectangular draped garments including Japanese kimonos, North African kaftans, and Greek chitons, and his long, tubular chemise silhouette became the template for 1920s dresses. During the 1910s dresses were worn with high sashes, which moved to the newly fashionable low hip level during the 1920s. His superb velvet evening coats (some with bold Raoul Dufy block prints on ivory velvet) wrapped and draped around the body. He repeated the cocoon-shaped evening coat in a variety of sumptuous fabrics.

Poiret loved printed fabrics, particularly the rose motif, commissioning Paul Iribe to design a silk which the Lyonnais silk manufacturer, Bianchini-Férier, made. Iribe's rose adorned his woven satin labels from around 1908 onward. The rare earlier label (1903–8) just bears the legend "Paul Poiret, rue Pasquier 37, Paris".

Heavily influenced by Diaghilev's *Ballets Russes*, Poiret's clothes often incorporated vivid colour combinations. When Léon Bakst's orientalist designs for the ballet *Scheherazade* premiered in Paris in 1910, Poiret embraced the discordant but brilliant colour combinations such as purple with orange or shocking pink with blue, in reaction to the tame, ladylike pastel shades especially popular with his rival Lucile.

Poiret's eveningwear became a riot of richly coloured damasks, velvets, and lamés. His early clothes are often crudely finished on the inside (those from the 1920s onward are typically well finished and of couture standard), but outside they are a glorious and often eclectic mixture of embroidery, lamé, velvet, and satin. This theatricality and exuberance set him apart along with his love of the Orient, exemplified by exotic textiles and couture turbans.

The "Sorbet" dress (1913), of ivory and black satin, embroidered with seed-beaded roses, with a hooped ring suspending the hem, had a contrasting obi-style cummerbund worn at the raised waistline and harem-style pantaloons or draped skirt. Owing to the nature of these lampshade gowns with circular skirts, only three seem to have survived – in the Victoria & Albert Museum, FIT New York, and the Chicago Historical Society.

Widely imitated, especially in America (complete with fake labels), Poiret eventually launched his own cheaper line in 1917. Alongside Lucile, he was one of the first couturiers to embrace American licensing agreements, encouraged by the decline of his couture business in the 1920s. He publicly denounced Coco Chanel's comfortable cardigan ensembles as *pauvreté de luxe* (luxurious poverty) (ironically she espoused the liberty and comfort he had pioneered). Declared bankrupt in 1928, he designed freelance for Printemps and Liberty but found it difficult to produce clothes within a budget. The glory days of the "King of Fashion" – with his lavish parties, prestigious fashion house, lifestyle stores, perfumes, and world-famous art collection – were well and truly over. His wonderful clothes remind us of his genius and are some of the most beautiful and desirable of all haute couture.

Below top to bottom, "Paul Poiret a Paris" label with Iribe rose. French comedian Cora Laparcerie wearing a "Lampshade" dress as "Le Minaret". Poiret's wife, the model Denise Poiret (née Boulet), wore the first version to his 1911 "Thousand and Second Night" party. The overdress and harem pants were completed with an aigrette-spiked turban.

PAUL POIRET

Below, Paul Poiret orientalist dress of bronze lamé, *c.*1922. The fabric has been gently draped and caught into an elaborately embroidered and beaded medallion. <u>W</u>

"Am I a fool when I dream of putting art into my dresses, a fool when I say that dressmaking is an art?" *Paul Poiret*

Right, Model posing as a caryatid wearing an embroidered tunic fastened with an appliqué-decorated belt over a chiffon dress by Lucile, 1912.

LUCILE

Above, Jade green velvet evening gown, *c*.1912–13. N

Lucile (or Lady Duff-Gordon) (1863–1935) was a pioneering businesswoman. She understood the importance of the American market early, establishing thriving couture establishments in New York and Chicago as well as licensing agreements with Sears, Roebuck to sell affordable ranges using mail-order catalogues.

Well connected, amusing, and creative, this "it girl" has become something of a cult figure. She began her career as a London dressmaker, trading as Mrs Lucy Wallace, then Maison Lucile in the 1890s, Madame Lucile, and finally just Lucile – her aristocratic title (she married Sir Cosmo Duff-Gordon in 1900) particularly helped sales in the United States.

She christened her "gowns of emotion" with evocative names such as "Love While You May" or "The Elusive Joy of Youth". Layers of filmy fabrics, often with pale pink charmeuse lining suggesting nudity, formed highly feminine, frothy gowns, with elaborate trimmings of metal-strip embroideries, silver braid, silk ribbon rosebuds, or frothy layers of lace. She also liked fur as a trim when the mood took her. In contrast, while working, she wore plain black wool jersey gowns. Her talented assistants included Howard Greer and Edward Molyneux. A young Norman Hartnell submitted designs for her approval that she stole and published as her own!

By 1912 Lucile's clients included royalty, celebrities, and society hostesses. Her international businesses were thriving when she and her husband sailed on the *Titanic*. They survived the disaster, but accusations that Sir Cosmo had bribed crew for a lifeboat place ruined their reputation. During the 1920s, her frivolous, charming, highly embellished creations fell out of favour, and between 1921 and 1924 her fashion houses closed and she became bankrupt. Her subsequent "Court Dressmaker" fashion house (opened 1928) survived only four years.

Anything by Lucile is highly desirable, but the gossamer-fine chiffons and silks are often in poor or fragile condition. Their rarity, romance, allure, and sheer femininity, combined with the designer's extraordinary life, make them extremely sought after by fashion historians and *Titanic* collectors alike.

"I was the first dressmaker to bring joy and romance into clothes, I was a pioneer." *Lucile*

Mariano Fortuny's clothes are timeless, artisanal creations that are as wearable now as when first made. Initially worn by artistic types and avant-garde beauties who wished to dress outside the mainstream of fashion, they are whisper-light, soft, and voluptuous.

Born to an affluent family in Granada, Spain, Mariano Fortuny (1871–1949) inherited his father's love of fine art and textiles and was an accomplished inventor, scientist, painter, sculptor, architect, lighting engineer, and photographer. He moved to Venice at 18, remaining there for the rest of his life. "The Magician of Venice" began experimenting with textiles in 1907. The "Delphos" dress was a column of goffered, pleated silk with neck and shoulder drawstrings and side seams adorned with handmade beads (whose weight held the dress in place). An optional belt, stencilled in silver or gold, could also be worn. The dresses were sleeveless, short sleeved, or with long slim sleeves finished along the outside edges with beautiful beads. The rarer, pleated silk dress, the "Peplos", had an integral over-tunic falling in beaded points to the sides. The silks (ranging from ivory to pitch black through pinks, blues, greens, rich purples, golden apricots, and deep cinnamons) were all hand-dyed with delicate vegetable dyes in Fortuny's home studio at the Palazzo Orfei.

Presumably pink-gold tones were the most popular, because they have survived in larger numbers, and richer, more unusual colours are generally more prized than pastel tones. The dresses did not change stylistically from 1910 to 1930 and can be difficult to date accurately. They are usually stamped with the Fortuny name on the belt (if that still survives) or along the inside selvedge edges of the side seams or underarm tapes. For summer, Fortuny also produced stencilled silk-gauze "Knossos" over-tunics in contrasting colours.

His sumptuous velvets and silks show true genius. He made entire wall hangings and furnishing textiles as well as jackets, coats, and dresses of stencilled silk. The designs were generally after the Antique, and taken from his lace and textiles collections. His velvet dresses stencilled in gold and silver with side seams and inner sleeves inset with pleated, goffered silk are highly valuable and desirable, combining the pleating of a "Delphos" with the fabulous velvet. These Renaissance-style gowns usually bear circular printed labels, as do his coats and jackets. His domino capes and panelled, stencilled jackets are also among his most desirable pieces.

Imitators and influences

Enormously popular in America, during the 1920s Fortuny moved production to a specially designed factory on the Giudecca. Fortuny soon attracted imitators such as the Rome-based Maria Monaci Gallenga (1880–1940) whose stencilling is usually in silver and gold on velvet. Her designs tend to be smaller-scaled and highly imaginative but without the same depth in tone and a harder, more regular pile to the velvet. She also used glass beads to edge her garments and sometimes signed her name within the velvet print. The Babani fashion house in Paris also made tunics, simple silk chiton-like dresses, and kaftan-like coats, but tended to adorn them with fine chain stitch in gold and silver threads rather than stencilling.

Fortuny gowns are instantly recognizable and mark out the wearer as someone of wealth, taste, and style. Body heat can cause the pleats to irreversibly loosen at the underarms and seat, and the tissue-fine silk falls prey to sharp heels, so hems must be examined for even the smallest of holes. Any damage reduces the value dramatically.

The 1960s and 1970s saw a renewed interest in Fortuny with several important retrospectives. Fortuny was an artist whose meticulous eye and glorious sense of colour, though imitated, have never been matched.

Below, Stencilled black silk evening coat, *c.*1910–20, with circular label (pictured): stencilled in gold with foliate traceries. The wide panelled sleeves are linked by striped glass Murano beads. R

MARIANO FORTUNY

Below, Stencilled red velvet jacket, *c.*1920–30: with circular label, of long, slim-fitting oriental shape, with pointed, curved cuffs, piped in grey and fastened by striped grey Murano beads. P

Right, Salmon-pink short-sleeved "Delphos" gown, *c.*1920–30: the inner selvedge printed "Fabriqué en Italie. Fortuny Deposé. Made in Italy"; the shoulders laced with cords adorned with Murano beads. S

"The fabrics are exquisite, the colours such as painters love, the lines such as sculptors admire." *American socialite Belle Whitney on Fortuny*

The late 19th century and early 20th saw an invasion of "Dollar Princesses" – rich, attractive daughters of wealthy American entrepreneurs intent on a titled husband (often land-rich and cash-poor).

There were a number of notable alliances. Jennie Jerome agreed to marry dashing young MP Lord Randolph Churchill after just three days; Consuelo Vanderbilt became Duchess of Marlborough; Mary Goelet, Duchess of Roxburghe; and Consuelo Yznaga, Duchess of Manchester; while the sewing-machine heiress Winnaretta Singer married the French Prince de Polignac. However, Mary Leiter (1870–1906), the daughter of a Chicago retail magnate, arguably won the most glittering prize, marrying George Curzon, the eldest son of Lord Scarsdale and Viceroy of India.

Mary Leiter was known for her beauty, intellect, and fashion sense. The couple secretly became engaged and were duly married in Washington, D.C. in 1895. He presented her with the Kedleston diamonds and her bridal gown was made by her favourite fashion house – Worth of Paris. Of ivory satin trimmed with antique lace, and with a long train, it was described as "simplicity itself" by the *Chicago Tribune*. Maison Worth, one of the most expensive of all the couture houses, was famed for its lavish embellishments and always used the finest silks, so its apparent "simplicity" was probably quite the opposite.

At the state ball celebrating the coronation of King Edward VII, Mary – now Vicereine of India – wore a truly magnificent Worth gown that has since come to be known as the "Peacock" dress.

Left and below, Mary Victoria Leiter, Marchioness Curzon in her Peacock Gown, 1909 (oil on canvas), by William Logsdail (1859–1944). Maison Worth produced the famous "Peacock" dress in Paris, and it was embroidered to shape by Indian craftsmen. The cloth of gold ground was completely covered in a shimmer of embroidered and beaded peacock feathers, the eyes formed from blue and green beetle wings. "Reville & Rossiter" woven satin label to waistband of ice blue 1911 dress. *Opposite left to right*, Striped purple velvet gown, *c.*1905, with tapelace-inserted bodice and trained skirt. L. Reville & Rossiter silver-brocaded ice blue satin ball gown, *c.*1911; the bodice adorned with reticella-like silver chemical lace, spangled with rhinestones. Originally worn by Mrs Lewis Harcourt, one of the "Dollar Princesses". M. Callot Sœurs sequinned lace ball gown, *c.*1908: edged in cream Bedfordshire Maltese lace and tapelace. L

Style Icon

BARONESS CURZON OF KEDLESTON

"In England, the American woman was looked upon as a strange and abnormal creature with habits and manners something between a red Indian and a Gaiety Girl." *Dollar Princess Jennie Jerome*

Reville & Rossiter Ltd 15-Hanover Square-W.

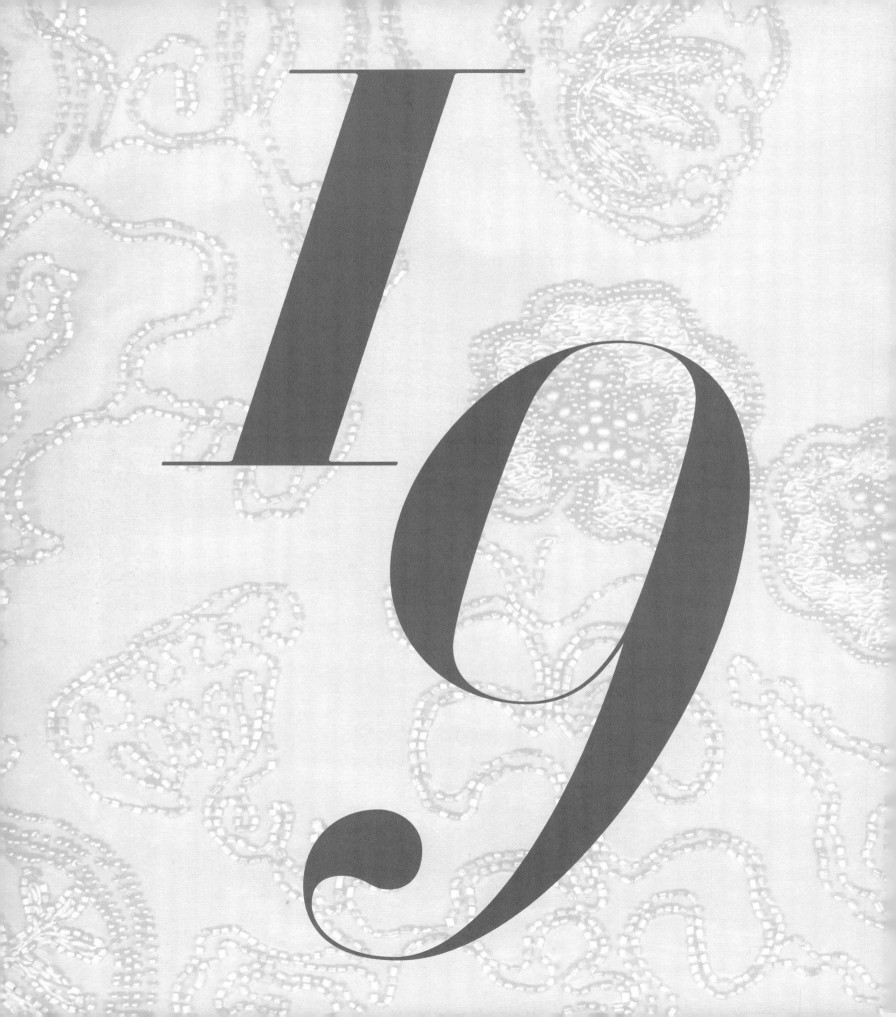

An era of decadence, exuberance, and celebration after the devastation of the Great War, the 1920s was the decade of the naughty flapper. She chopped her long tresses into a neat, polished little bob, smoked cigarettes from long holders, twirled her beads, and did the Charleston to the latest jazz song on her portable wind-up record player. The tight corsets, tiny waists, heaving bosoms, and layers of lace and petticoats of the Edwardian period were banished in favour of the *garçonne* look, no longer hourglass but cylindrical. Suntans were popularized by Coco Chanel, and the aesthetic was sporty, boyish, and youthful, though the older generation still dressed in what were, in essence, Edwardian fashions.

Silhouettes focused on the hem and waistline. As breasts and real waists vanished, the eye was drawn to the ankles and – as the decade progressed and hemlines shortened – to the legs. In the early 1920s dresses for day and evening were just above the ankle or very low on the calf and the waistline was very slightly lowered. By 1922 the waist had dropped to hip level with side swags, floating panels, and drapes. The discovery of Tutankhamun's tomb in 1923 inspired beautiful, beaded, Egyptian-themed dresses, often with little pharaohs and hieroglyphs as decoration. The other great craze was for chinoiserie, and real embroidered Chinese jackets and coats were worn for evening, as well as haute couture dresses made in the orientalist style by designers such as Poiret, Patou, and Callot. By 1925 the hem had risen to below the knee and some designers such as Patou were reintroducing the hint of a natural waist. By 1926 most skirts rested comfortably on the knee reflecting women's increased emancipation. From 1927 to 1928 the skirts became more flared and the dropped-level waist was more of a focus, with hems often dipping at the sides, or with longer "peacock tail" rear hems and irregular hemlines. By 1929 hemlines were longer, of irregular lengths, and often incorporated pretty handkerchief pleats.

Eveningwear used richly coloured velvets and crêpes de Chine, and beading, sequins, and embroidery against a solid-coloured ground were used throughout the decade. Despite their weight, such dresses allowed ease of movement and acted as canvases for the wonderful geometric art deco patterns that were in vogue. Although these lavishly beaded and embroidered dresses could be expensive (especially the haute couture examples embroidered by Lesage), in Paris there was a huge industry turning out ready-to-wear versions. These have survived in quite large numbers, mainly because, instead of using the more expensive silk and chiffon grounds (which have often fallen apart owing to the weight of the beads), they have muslin grounds that are much more sturdy and forgiving. These carry small red and white woven "Made in France" labels and, if flamboyant art deco designs, they can still be quite pricey. The single-coloured beaded dresses are still relatively affordable.

By the mid-1920s lamés and metallic weaves, sometimes in combination with a floral print, were popular. Patterned cut velvets, with a chiffon ground, were used for both evening dresses and opera capes. Capes

Below left, Bakelite faux-jade art deco vanity case and an ivory cigarette holder with green painted tip. C

Below, Sequined cobweb-patterned dress with "peacock tail" hem *c.*1927–8: although ready-to-wear, it is still spectacular. L

THE ROARING TWENTIES

"All we were saying was, 'Tomorrow we may die, so let's get drunk and make love.'" *Lois Long*

Right, Illustration showing a young lady out walking, wearing a white crêpe dress and multicoloured Moroccan-style cardigan jacket by Jean Patou, 1924.

and coats had large, often padded collars or were trimmed with fur.

By day, knitted silk or jersey two-piece ensembles were very popular often with art deco motifs incorporated into them, with simple pleated skirts. Humble cardigans and sweaters with a plain skirt were produced by couture houses such as Chanel and Patou, whose sports-inspired day clothes also increasingly influenced their eveningwear.

The creators

The main labels to look for are Chanel, Patou, Lanvin, Vionnet, Callot, Louiseboulanger, Prémet, Molyneux, Gallenga, Fortuny, Augustabernard, and, to a lesser degree, Paquin, Doucet, Chéruit, and Worth. Paul Poiret, who had reigned supreme in the opening decade of the century, was unable to modernize or adapt his opulent, expensive designs and was no longer a major player.

Accessories

The little cloche hat was worn in one form or another right through the decade, and into the early 1930s. Brightly coloured gloves became popular toward the end of the decade. For day, a leather clutch with matching shoes in two-tone leather or lizard skin was required; for the evening, a pretty soft velvet purse with moulded celluloid mounts or enamelled and gem-set art deco-style mount and clasp. Evening shoes in metallic brocades, gold or silver leather, or richly coloured satin were fastened by a single button. Some of the shoes in the late 1920s had rhinestone-studded Bakelite heels. Little parasols and umbrellas often coordinated the look. Richly embroidered and fringed Spanish or Cantonese shawls and large celluloid hair combs lent an air of exoticism as did Egyptian metallic-stamped Azute stoles with their shimmering geometric patterns against a silk mesh ground. Long strings of beads broke up the bodice line on a dress and long droplet earrings drew attention to the head. Slave bangles adorned the bare sleeveless arms and wrists. Fans were popular for evening – either ostrich plume, sequined gauze, or printed paper. Boudoir caps of fine lace with ribbon-work flowers were worn in bed to help keep the shingled and bobbed hairstyles in place.

Below left to right, Two tone leather day shoes. Each C. A knitted wine silk ensemble, ready-to-wear, *c.*1925, with strong art deco abstract motifs. It came with matching knickers and petticoat. F

Right, Beaded crêpe de Chine flapper dress, *c.*1922, ombré-dyed and beaded with large scale gold palmettes. Note the just-above-the-ankle length. D

Below right, Rare Prémet couture black crêpe de Chine dress, *c.*1926, with gold ribbon bands and "peasant" embroidery. These rarely appear on the market. <u>L</u>

Right, Long narrow silk scarves were popular accessories in the 1920s. Each <u>A</u>

JEAN PATOU

Above, Jean Patou in New York selecting American models to take back to Paris to model his clothes. Six girls were chosen from the hundreds who turned up outside *Vogue*'s New York offices in December 1924.

Handsome, debonair, and (unusually in fashion even then) heterosexual, Jean Patou (1880–1936) cut a dash in the world of Parisian couture at a time when it was largely dominated by women.

Like the man himself, his clothes were unfussy, well cut, and effortlessly stylish. He skilfully combined colours and commissioned exclusive silk dyes each season (including the deep violet Patou blue). In 1922 he became the first designer to use a logo on the outside of his clothes – "JP" was emblazoned on breast pockets and bodices as an integral decoration of his knitwear and dresses, declaring to the world that this "little nothing" of a dress had come from an expensive couture house.

Patou admitted he didn't have a clue about dressmaking. Like many studios today, he had a "laboratory" of designers, but he always made the final edit and the collections maintained his distinctive look. His signature style was "sporty" – featuring clean, simple lines, clever seaming, pleats in skirts, and unfussy decoration, all of which gave ease of movement. He produced wonderful twinset knits with Cubist-style patterns and equally striking beachwear. The French Riviera had become a major summer resort and the knitted fabrics used for his swimwear (designed both for active swimming and just looking nice) were tested to make sure they didn't shrink in salt water. Deemed humble and unimportant, few of these innovative costumes have survived, which now makes them rare and important.

The American market

Patou made a fortune in America, where his clothes suited the taller, athletic, rangy women. To appeal to this market he selected six US models to take to Paris in a major publicity coup. So the US is likely to be a happy hunting ground for collectors today.

His last ground-breaking collection was in 1929 when he restored the waistline to the natural level and his knee-length skirts descended in length, with handkerchief points and irregular, graduated hems. It successfully sounded the death knell of the *garçonne* – the curvaceous, feminine siren was back.

Despite the designer's popularity, Patou pieces of the 1920s (which museums clamour for) are scarce and anything by him incorporating his strong, sporty aesthetic is particularly desirable. Thirties gowns seem to have survived in greater numbers (the house continued after his death) and are therefore more accessible price-wise.

Right, Jean Patou soft pink velvet evening cape with label, mid-1920s, faced and lined in pink satin. <u>G</u>

Far right, Jean Patou rose crêpe de Chine, fringed cocktail dress, *c.*1927. Unlabelled with degradé pointed bands of beige pink fringing. <u>G</u>

Baba d'Erlanger (1901–45) was an "it girl" of the 1920s, the daughter of the French-born but naturalized British banker Baron d'Erlanger and his eccentric wife, Catherine. "Baba" (Liliane was her real name) had an unusual childhood, growing up in Lord Byron's old house in London. Her mother dressed in medieval-inspired fashions or as a nun entirely in white, but often dressed her daughter in gold. A six-foot turbaned Egyptian attendant accompanied Baba to ballet classes and, unsurprisingly, she grew up with very individual taste in clothes and style.

Slender, willowy, and with a beautiful oval face, Baba was the ideal of the *garçonne* look. She outlined her eyes with black kohl and greased her upper lids (occasionally adding glitter too). Her lips were outlined in deep crimson, she wore maroon nail polish, and her sculpted black bob didn't have a hair out of place. She was great friends with fellow "it girls" – Paula Gellibrand and Romanov princess Natalia Pavlovna Paley – and was part of the international *beau monde* that included Cecil Beaton, the Mitford and Curzon sisters, Daisy Fellowes, Elsie de Wolfe (Lady Mendl), and Oliver Messel. She dressed at Chanel (who was also a friend) and at Lucien Lelong (to whom Princess Natalia was married). She was severe in her fashion choices, preferring monochrome, minimal outfits for day to emphasize her slender figure and pale face.

In 1923 she married the French prince Jean-Louis de Faucigny-Lucinge, who described her as "exotically beautiful". They hosted some of the most famous parties of the postwar years. Baba spent the rest of her short life bringing up her family, organizing world-famous parties, and looking super-stylish.

Style Icon

BABA D'ERLANGER

"One of the most elegant women in Paris." *Jean-Louis de Faucigny-Lucinge*

Below left to right, Striking ready-to-wear beaded flapper dress, *c.*1928, labelled "Made in France": the beige muslin ground with gold and black bugle-beaded designs; hem pointed to the sides. H. Cut velvet opera cape and a gold cord wig studded with rhinestones, 1920s, the cape labelled "Made in Paris for Saks & Company": the art deco lozenge patterned velvet changes from pale beige at the neck to deep cinnamon at the hem. Cape E, wig L

Right, Princess Jean-Louis de Faucigny-Lucinge, aka Baba, photographed in 1929 wearing a Suzanne Talbot close fitting black felt hat with winged sides adorned with a brooch.

One of the most influential designers of the 1920s and 1930s, Jeanne Lanvin (1867–1946) is indisputably also one of the great couturiers.

Her career spanned the 1880s to the 1940s and her signature design was the *robe de style*, which she made throughout the 1920s irregardless of what was happening in mainstream fashion. This can make precisely dating them difficult. The Italian Renaissance, religion, the Middle Ages, India, China, and Japan all served as inspirations, and her 1922 beaded medieval-style ivory silk gown was even copied by the English court dressmaker Madame Handley-Seymour for the wedding dress of the Duchess of York, the future Queen Elizabeth, the Queen Mother

Exquisite embellishment

Lanvin was a genius at decorating carefully chosen fabrics. The square, diamond, oval, and round sequins on her clothes merit close inspection; there can be textured or crimped edges and mixed sizes, textures, and shapes in one garment. Antique and oriental textiles inspired her embroidery, and ribbons, chenille, gilded leather, and beads were employed to great effect. But shape and construction were equally important. The

Below and bottom, A robe de style: panniered, organza, or taffeta gowns with integral hoops and highly embellished by ruffles, sequins, appliqué, and embroidery. Despite prevailing gamine fashions, there was a demand for something more romantic and frivolous. Z. Haute couture label with mother and child motif designed by Armand Albert Rateau. These appear in adult clothes from Winter 1919 onwards.

*Below right, A Jeanne Lanvin blue satin and lace robe de style, c.*1923. J. *Opposite*, Model Marjorie Willis, seen from behind, wearing a black taffeta dress with a large butterfly bow by Lanvin, and with a rhinestone brooch at the centre back, 1927.

"Grand Old Lady" of haute couture remained cutting edge throughout her career, producing beautiful, highly wearable, and elegant clothes. Her 1930s sheaths (sometimes with cropped kimono-like sleeves, or sexy halter-neck bodices above hip-hugging crêpe skirts) were as contemporary as anything produced by younger designers. Upon her death, her daughter, the Comtesse de Polignac, took over the business and from 1963 employed the Spanish couturier Antonio Castillo, whose designs are also very desirable. Employing "new blood" has kept Lanvin alive, a tradition continued by Alber Elbaz in the early 2000s.

It remains possible to buy simple, unadorned (or fur-trimmed) twenties and thirties coats and capes relatively cheaply. However, dresses with fabulous embroidery and beadwork can command five-figure sums, especially the quintessential *robes de style* (often made of delicate silk taffeta or organza, many have perished). Her sexy sheath gowns are in demand with buy-to-wear and museum clients alike. If they have avant-garde elements, such as cropped kimono sleeves, white-on-black abstract appliqués or major embroidery and beadwork, they are most desirable and hotly contested at auction.

JEANNE LANVIN

Left, Coco Chanel in 1926 wearing a comfortable but stylish cardigan suit with matching beret and masses of costume jewellery. She was her own best advertisement for seemingly effortless chic.

Top to bottom, Label from a day dress, *c.*1918; label on a late-1920s cape; label on a 1926 beaded dress.

CHANEL IN THE TWENTIES

"She wore a slipover jersey sweater and a tweed skirt and her hair brushed back like a boy's. She started all that." *Ernest Hemingway*

Coco Chanel (1883–1971) once said of herself: "Chanel is a style. A mode becomes demoded. Style never does." As usual, Coco was right and her signature style has never been unfashionable. Like Patou, her day clothes were sporty and practical, in light-as-a-feather crêpe de Chine, wool crêpe, or jersey. She used the best fabrics. A typical day dress could be fairly plain with a little tie at the neck or a tiered, graduated skirt. However, the finishing is second to none, with all interior seams meticulously over-sewn by hand and the raw edges of the silk or chiffon picot-trimmed to perfection. Like Balenciaga, whom she admired, she was obsessed with how a sleeve fitted into the garment, spending hours fiddling with the setting until she was satisfied. If she used a printed floral chiffon fabric for a dress, she would often have the individual flower heads cut out and appliquéd onto a matching coat or jacket, or she would have them picot-edged and layered and turn them into three-dimensional floral corsages. It is these careful, minute details that set her clothes apart.

Chanel took inspiration from the world around her and made the seemingly ordinary extraordinary. From working fishermen and *matelots*, she took the striped Breton top and reefer jacket, teamed with wide-legged trousers that buttoned at the sides, creating a revolutionary look for a woman in the late 1920s. From workmen, she took patterned neckerchiefs and white cotton jackets. Her lover, the Duke of Westminster, showered her with expensive jewellery (which she mixed with costume jewels), took her sailing on his yacht (where she wore Breton tops, *matelot* trousers, and naval-style berets with grosgrain bands), and invited her on salmon fishing trips to Scotland where she became quite adept at the sport and developed her love of Scottish tartans, Fair Isle patterned

knitwear, tweeds, and wools. She borrowed elements from his hunting, shooting, and fishing clothes; men's cardigans, waistcoats, shirts with cufflinks, tweeds, and trousers were all incorporated into her wardrobe and collections throughout her career.

Chanel set up a factory at Asnières-sur-Seine, on the outskirts of Paris, for machine-knitted jerseys and silks. The Russian Futurist poet Iliazd was responsible for the colour and texture of the weaves, producing art deco tapestry-patterned and striped knits that she turned into cardigan suits and dresses. Owning the factory gave her control of quality and ensured exclusivity. Her use of these humble fabrics led the couturier Paul Poiret to describe this look derisively as *pauvreté de luxe* (luxurious poverty). By the late 1920s she went on to produce printed silks. Probably because they were so comfortable and wearable, the majority of these informal ensembles wore out or fell prey to moths – and so are rare today and very desirable.

In the late teens and early 1920s for day, and particularly for evening, she used Russian- or Egyptian-style embroidery on her clothes, opening her own workshop and employing aristocratic Russian émigrées, including Grand Duchess Maria Pavlova (who later set up her own business, Kitmir, producing colourful embroideries using a chain-stitch machine for larger-scale production). These ethnic embroidered dresses are rare, but there is one in the collection of the Metropolitan Museum of Art, New York. She also adored lace, using heavy guipure, in pastel shades, ivory, and black – in everything from slender flapper styles with dropped waistlines to full-skirted dance gowns – right up to the 1950s.

In 1926 Coco launched the perfect backdrop for jewels, real or fake – the little black dress, which became the staple of every woman's wardrobe. She usually relied on clever construction and textures achieved by sequins, embroidery, appliqués, beadwork, or lace for maximum impact on the LBDs. American *Vogue* wittily described these luxurious, understated clothes with the strapline "Here is a Ford signed by Chanel". They were universally appealing, high quality, and widely imitated (which she didn't mind, feeling that a designer had not really "made it" until their designs filtered down to street level), but hers were set apart by the quality.

Market

Chanel is unique because, while her really early pieces from the 1920s and 1930s are highly desirable and valuable (regularly commanding five-figure sums at auction, from museums and collectors who would never dream of wearing them), even boutique ready-to-wear pieces from the present time are popular at auction, as buy-to-wear clients vie with one another. Likewise, costume jewellery from all periods is highly collectable as are the signature quilted-leather handbags and two-tone pumps. She was a remarkable woman and the fact that, a century after she first began designing, women are still clamouring for her classic style is a true testament of her greatness.

Below, Rare Chanel couture "ribbon" dress, *c*.1924, of black crêpe de Chine, with bugle bead "ribbon" zigzag fringes falling in four crêpe georgette tiers to the skirt. V

Below, Rare Coco Chanel couture printed lace cocktail gown, Spring/Summer 1928, comprising: ivory crêpe de Chine slip with attached skirt panel of lace, and short over-bodice with scarf-like panel to one shoulder edged in ruffles of appliquéd lace flower heads. W

Right, Chanel tiered white lace dress with silver beaded spangles, accessorized with a large tulle fan and Delman shoes, 1928.

After the bugle-beaded razzamatazz of the 1920s, global economic recession in the 1930s made flaunting wealth socially unacceptable and there was a move toward sophisticated simplicity. Vionnet is credited with inventing the bias cut that makes this period's masterful constructions so special. Other notable designers are Elsa Schiaparelli, Coco Chanel, Jeanne Paquin, Mainbocher, Jeanne Lanvin, Jean Patou, Augustabernard, Lucien Lelong, Robert Piguet, Marcel Rochas, Jacques Heim, Nina Ricci, Balenciaga, Molyneux, Hartnell, Adrian, and Charles James.

Designers played with colour contrasts and with strong graphic art deco prints. Tweed, jersey, printed floral chiffon, satin, and crêpe de Chine were popular for daywear, with metallic weaves, brocade, richly coloured velvet and chiffon, cloqué silk, satin, frilled, layered tulle, shimmering sequins, wool crêpe, striped or patterned rayon, and artificial silk in eveningwear. Paris couture also included novelty fabrics such as spun glass. Lace (adored by Chanel) was very popular.

The look

The look was long and lean, languid and serene. Shingled, jaw-length, side- or centre-parted hair framed the face or was slicked back with curls at the nape of the neck. Toward the end of the decade, hair was swept up, curled onto the front of the crown, and often held in a chignon with a velvet snood.

Dramatic evening make-up paired shaded, glossed eyelids with plucked or drawn-in eyebrows and cupid's-bow lips.

Day looks were efficient and pretty, featuring well-tailored, low to mid-calf-length suits or dresses, floral chiffon garden party gowns with integral or matching bolero jackets, and pretty blouses with elaborate jabot frills, large neck bows, lace collars, and feature-buttons in novelty shapes, with florals, or angular art deco Lucite. Trousers, pioneered by Greta Garbo and Chanel, were increasingly popular but advocated by *Vogue* only in 1939. In Europe and America there was a general move toward comfortable sports-influenced clothing for practical daywear as well as a focus on specialist ensembles for various activities – including extremely fine ski-suits, golf, tennis, hiking, and yachting ensembles – and knitted costumes, halter-neck tops, shorts, and slinky satin pyjamas for the beach.

Modest and demure by day, a girl could transform into a Greta Garbo, Ginger Rogers, or Jean Harlow-style vamp for evening. Figure-hugging, bias-cut gowns left little to the imagination, especially if made of satin or clinging crêpe. The leggy emphasis of the 1920s shifted to the torso and a long lean silhouette, embodied by Jean Harlow.

Vionnet, Alix Grès, and other Parisian couturiers advocated the classic "goddess" look of Greek-inspired draped gowns in ivory or

Below left to right, Hermès red leather clutch bag, 1930s: the interior stamped in gold "Hermès, 24 FbSt.Honoré, Paris", with silvered lifter-clasp. F. Day dress, possibly Jean Patou, *c*.1935, in black wool with contrasting red trim; complex knotted tie to neck. G

Right, Coco Chanel manages to make her male companion (the Duke of Laurino) look very underdressed on the Lido beach in 1930. Coco wears her *matelot*-style trousers, jewelled naval-style cap, cuff, and ropes of pearls.

THE SOPHISTICATED THIRTIES

"Bare your bosom as low as your figure or modesty will allow." *Vogue*

pastel-toned jersey or crêpe, with little or no adornment. Slenderness was a key ingredient and magazines reported on how "silly women are still starving themselves into hysteria".

The silhouette

The 1930 waistline was just below the ribcage, with the close-fitting skirt flaring out below the knee through the use of godets, thereby elongating the legs and torso. Bolero jackets or capelets of feathers, sequins, and matching fabrics shifted attention to the shoulders and made the waist and hips seem even smaller. Belts with art deco Bakelite buckles, paste-inset clasps, or contrasting sashes also drew attention to the waist. Ingeniously designed sleeves that could be puffed, flounced, or of layered tulle, wide raglan, Magyar, or bishop-shaped, became a feature. Backs descended further with weighted cowl necks. Camiknickers, French knickers, and camisoles became popular under the closely fitting evening gowns.

As economic depression lifted in 1935, Lanvin produced stunning halter-neck gowns with sequined bodices and crêpe bias-cut skirts, and bustle and rear bow effects shifted the focus to the derrière. Frills and flounces prevailed, with the introduction of romantic, big-skirted crinoline gowns and high-waisted empire line and ruched bodices in 1936 as skirt trains shortened. Opera coats or capes had large, padded, or fur-trimmed collars, ruched detailing, and interestingly shaped sleeves. By 1937 breasts were high and pointed and stomachs flat, with ever more pronounced and boxy shoulders.

With the outbreak of World War II in 1939, clothes shed their frills and frippery. Rayon, taffeta, satin, moss crêpe, wool, and damask were used often in muted, dark colours or bold stripes, though tulle crinoline dresses, puff sleeves, and boleros continued to be popular. Suits had longer jackets fitted to the hips with day skirts just below the knee. Basques drew the eye to natural hips and waist, but strapless dresses with integral corsets and full skirts foreshadowed the New Look.

Accessories

Belts drew attention back to waists. Long slim scarves and handkerchiefs adorned necks, and fur (particularly ermine) capes, stoles, coats, and muffs were common.

Day shoes had low, slender heels that became higher for evening. Metallic sandals with covered toes were also popular. Leather gloves with decorative gauntlets were worn for day and long satin or kid gloves for the evening. Oblong leather clutches had art deco fastenings for daytime, while pretty evening bags of velvet, brocade, or petit point sported jewelled clasps.

Costume jewellery was prevalent – large showy bangles, ropes of beads or pearls, and art deco jewelled clips on bodices were all popular. Hat styles included the tricorn, pointed airman's cap, beret worn far back, low-crowned straw with drooping brim, all intended to make the head appear small and neat. Later, turbans and higher-crowned hats with veils were worn. Summer hats were often large and wide-brimmed.

Below left, Pair of gold brocaded and leather dance shoes. B

Below, Jeanne Lanvin's version of the "goddess gown": late 1930s or early 1940s, of draped black silk jersey. L

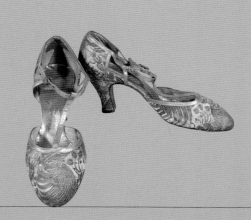

Below, Pink satin-backed crêpe bias-cut sheath, in the style of Lanvin, *c.*1934, the long, trained skirt with finger loop. F

Right, Molyneux lace bias-cut dress with jewelled clasp to belt, 1931.

Elsa Schiaparelli's ethos was "that clothes had to be architectural: that the body must never be forgotten and it must be used as a frame is used in a building". She was a great self-publicist and produced avant-garde creations each season, preferring her gowns to be playful rather than merely tasteful. Simultaneously controversial and gorgeous, her collections always included wearable, elegant black dresses that could be teamed with an embroidered or appliquéd jacket or cape. She used metallic leather trimmings, (often combined with Swarovski crystals and beadwork from 1935 onward), as well as lavish embroidery by Lesage.

After periods living in London and New York, the vivacious and charismatic Italian-born Schiaparelli (1890–1973) entered Paris society. Her first creation, in 1927, was a *trompe-l'oeil* sweater, mimicking the fashionable neck bows on dresses and blouses. It caused a sensation at a society lunch and a buyer from Strauss department store in New York asked for 40 sweaters and 40 skirts to be delivered in just two weeks. Unable to knit herself, she commissioned an Armenian "peasant" couple to work up the sweaters, while her own dressmaker made up the skirts. They featured in French *Vogue* and, with no formal training, Schiaparelli found she was now in business.

Wool and the skilfully made, naturally dyed weaves of Scottish tartans feature heavily. The innovative "Mad Cap" – a tiny knitted tube cap that could be moulded into any shape – was copied by an American manufacturer who made a fortune. Schiaparelli, however, did not, and, after spotting the copy worn by a baby, she destroyed all of her own versions. She was the first to open a boutique alongside her couture salon, stocking costume jewellery, perfume, evening sweaters, skirts, blouses, and accessories (all trifles previously scorned by the haute couture houses). It became instantly famous and was widely copied by other couturiers.

In 1934 Schiaparelli opened a short-lived fashion house in London, which closed when war was declared. Identical to the French models, these "London"-labelled pieces occasionally appear in UK auctions, but Schiaparelli's clothes demanded women who didn't mind being singled out in a crowd and many British clients had conservative tastes.

Her 1935 couture designs included padlocks for suits, evening raincoats, spun-glass dresses, and buttons of French gold sovereigns. Buttons (many by the jeweller Jean Schlumberger) became a house speciality. Reasoning that the days of lady's maids were numbered, Schiaparelli also championed the use of zip fasteners for evening gowns, making large, chunky, coloured plastic zippers a key design feature. The dresses sold well, especially in the United States.

The Art of Fashion

Schiaparelli collaborated with some of the finest fashion photographers of the age, including Man Ray, George Hoyningen-Huene, Horst P. Horst, and Cecil Beaton. Christian ("Bébé") Bérard sketched her

Below left to right, "Shocking" perfume bottle (launched 1937): the shape was modelled on the torso of one of Schiaparelli's clients, Mae West. Schiaparelli was superstitious and the name of the perfume had to begin with the letter "S". C. Schiaparelli couture coat-dress, fair to poor condition, late 1930s–early 1940s, fastened by five detachable buttons formed from rocks of turquoise with gold mounts. M

Right, Schiaparelli in London in 1935 wearing her "trouser-skirt", examples of which she made for both day and evening in different fabrics. They were deemed outrageous by the press of the day. "They were graceful and feminine and to my mind much more modest than skirts," their designer said.

ELSA SCHIAPARELLI

"Dress designing is to me not a profession but an art."
Elsa Schiaparelli

designs, and Salvador Dalí helped her devise a coat like a chest of drawers (inspired by *The Anthropomorphic Cabinet*, 1936), a black hat in the form of a shoe with a shocking pink velvet heel, and another in the shape of a lamb-chop. Very few women had the nerve to wear these Surrealist designs and few were made, which makes them both rare and valuable. Dalí and Schiaparelli also collaborated on the colourful "Circus" collection of Spring 1938, and among their creations was a contrasting black satin "Skeleton" dress, padded and quilted with the outlines of bones. Despite the inevitable press coverage, there does not appear to be a surviving example and it would fetch six figures if discovered.

For Autumn/Winter 1937 two Jean Cocteau drawings featured on an evening coat and a grey linen jacket. These are among the most valuable and desirable pieces of haute couture ever made. That same year Schiaparelli introduced the shocking pink with which she became synonymous and her perfume of the same name. Celebrity clients included Mae West, Wallis Simpson, Gloria Swanson, Lauren Bacall, Claudette Colbert, Merle Oberon, Katherine Hepburn, Greta Garbo, and Marlene Dietrich.

She spent most of the war in America but her staff in Paris continued to create models based on previous collections. In 1945 she reopened to great acclaim and increasingly relied upon lucrative American licensing deals whereby menswear, fur coats, table linen, tailored suits, hats, shoes, and baby clothes were all made bearing her signature label but without her design input. These licensed products, though collectable, are of relatively low value. It is her couture Paris and London labels that are the real treasures. Schiaparelli continued producing successful collections until her retirement in 1954 when, ironically, her old rival, Chanel, decided to reopen.

Below left, Schiaparelli London black wool evening jacket, Winter 1936, lavishly embroidered in metal strip, gold thread, sequins, and beads. It was intended to be worn over a black crêpe dress and accessorized with a glycerined ostrich-feather cone hat – the perfect ensemble "for an evening of dinner, the cinema, cocktails, or cabaret". P

Below centre, Schiaparelli couture deep fuchsia velvet evening coat, late 1930s, "Paris" label, with dramatic fan-shaped pleats forming leg-o'-mutton sleeves. U

Below left, Schiaparelli camouflage brocaded gown, 1937–8, woven with shimmering iridescent gold Lurex threads in ripple effects, with black celluloid zip fasteners to the long sleeves. The gown shows her interest in, and use of, unusual fabrics. O

Below left to right, The famous Cocteau designs. Grey linen jacket embroidered by Lesage. EE. Purple silk coat. EE. Both Autumn/Winter 1937.

Undeniably one of the most stylish and controversial women of the 20th century, Wallis Simpson (1896–1986) appeared on the Best Dressed List for 40 years and her relationship with Edward VIII triggered a constitutional crisis. They married in 1937, when she wore a custom-designed, pale blue, crêpe Mainbocher gown with matching gloves (she always hated her hands).

When she entered a room every head turned – scouring her slim, elegant form to take in every detail, from the slick perfection of the hair, to the tips of her exquisite Perugia shoes. Her lips, defined in deep scarlet, contrasted with her pale complexion and dark hair, which emphasized the piercing blue of her eyes. By day she wore exquisitely tailored suits or simple dresses accessorized with embroidered gossamer scarves and leather handbags – all emblazoned with her monogram. Underneath, she wore the finest lingerie of sleek satin or diaphanous chiffon, bias-cut with embroidered monograms and lace insertions.

Her life, which she once described as "Wallis in Wonderland", was largely spent organizing the Duke's itinerary, preparing her appearance, shopping, arranging her famous dinner parties, and socializing. She regularly attended the couture collections and the major fashion houses vied for her custom. She patronized many, but her favourites in the 1930s were Mainbocher and Schiaparelli. Mainbocher created severe, elegant, no-nonsense lines, while Schiaparelli's ingenious, whimsical collections appealed to Wallis's sense of fun and impatience with convention.

Wallis was never a slave to fashion, knowing what best suited her and avoiding things that didn't. Marc Bohan of Dior, who designed the black organza gown she wore to attend the Duke's funeral in 1972, said of her: "She liked everything as plain as possible and that was my taste too." Stripped of superfluous detail and trimmings, her clothes acted as a backdrop to her dazzling jewels, specially commissioned by Edward. Sometimes he would take important antique family jewels, have them broken up for their stones, and remodelled especially for her. Many were engraved with secret messages or endearments in his handwriting.

There have been highly celebrated auctions of Wallis's belongings, and provenance will add at least a zero to any couture garment. Although her 1930s jewels have survived, her clothes from the period have never come up for auction. She donated her wedding dress to the Metropolitan Museum, New York, in 1950, but the fate of the rest of her early wardrobe remains a mystery. Perhaps it is meticulously wrapped in tissue somewhere, waiting for someone to discover it...

Style Icon

WALLIS SIMPSON

"My husband gave up everything for me ... I'm not a beautiful woman ... so the only thing I can do is dress better than anyone else." *Wallis Simpson*

What would Wallis wear? *Stylish understated clothes to enhance her willowy figure and show her jewels to best effect *Gloves *Monogrammed handbag with matching shoes *Opulent jewels by Cartier or Van Cleef & Arpels

Although Madeleine Vionnet (1876–1975) was highly acclaimed during her lifetime and acknowledged by fashion collectors and historians as one of the greatest designers, she is not a household name. Nonetheless, she possessed an unrivalled technical knowledge of fabric and construction.

Credited with inventing the bias cut in the 1920s (bias bands had traditionally been used to edge and bind necklines), she took whole panels of fabric and used complicated seam arrangements to take all the bulk away from a dress, allowing it to fit accurately and beautifully. Issey Miyake has written of Vionnet's clothes that they "are based on the dynamics of movement, and they never stray from this fundamental ideology".

A couture apprenticeship

Raised by her working-class father in a small town to the southwest of Paris, she became an apprentice to a seamstress at the age of 11 and was made *première* (responsible for overseeing the *mains* ("hands"), or in-house seamstresses) at Vincent & Cie, a small Paris fashion house, at 19. She joined the fashionable society dressmaker Kate Reilly (who specialized in copying French couture models) at 11–12 Dover Street, London in 1895, before taking up a post with the famous house of Callot Sœurs in 1901.

In 1906 Vionnet was tempted away by the couturier Jacques Doucet, who allowed her to create her own models in his fashion house. There she dispensed with the high-collared, skin-coloured jersey body sheaths that models wore when showing clothes, insisting her clothes be worn next to the skin. In 1912 she opened a small fashion house on the rue de Rivoli, producing gowns that were in keeping with the other major couture houses of the day, as her innovative cutting skills evolved. Very few gowns bearing the earliest woven satin label survive and none has ever come onto the open market.

When she reopened after World War I, she commissioned the famous Vionnet logo from the Italian Futurist artist and designer Thayaht. This label appeared from 1920 to 1939, sometimes accompanied by a printed thumbprint. Her first advertisements included stern warnings to copyists, and from 1921 her satin labels bore her actual inked thumbprint alongside the embroidered signature, "Madeleine Vionnet". These labels evolved into printed labels (complete with printed thumbprint) from the late 1920s.

In 1923 Vionnet moved to 50 avenue Montaigne and employed more than 200 people (rising to 1200 three years later), providing education to apprentices and free healthcare to the staff and their families. At Madeleine Vionnet Inc. New York (established 1924; closed 1932), Paris-made, ready-to-wear copies were sold because the American models did not meet the couturier's rigorous standards. Throughout the 1930s Vionnet's importance and influence grew. Her bias-cut gowns were admired and imitated but her genius in construction was never equalled. She finally closed her doors in 1939 and her assistants Jacques Griffe, Mad Maltezos, Suzie

Below, Vionnet lilac ombré chiffon bias-cut cocktail gown, *c.*1927, bearing green printed label with silver thumbprint, the skirt falling in gored handkerchief pleats. (Slightly altered at shoulders.) <u>P</u>

Right, Model wearing a Vionnet tiered white tulle ball gown, June 1935.

MADELEINE VIONNET – THE ARCHITECT OF COUTURE

"If a woman smiles, her dress must also smile." *Madeleine Vionnet*

Below right, Green cut velvet evening gown, Autumn/Winter 1937. U

Right, Early 1920s Vionnet embroidered label with real inked Vionnet thumbprint to prove the gown was an original.

Above, A rare Boris Lacroix for Madeleine Vionnet wine suede handbag, initialled in gilt metal "MV", 1930s. J

Carpentier, and Marcelle Chaumont opened their own prestigious houses. Griffe (whom she treated as a son) inherited some of her masterful cutting and construction techniques and, because of this, his creations are also highly desirable.

Working methods and designs

Madeleine Vionnet did not work from sketches, but with fabric on a 60cm (24 inch) tall figure, sizing the pieces up to fit the life-size form. Like Grès, she had an encyclopaedic knowledge of fabrics. Early 1920s clothes tended to be based on a rectangular shape and were cylindrical but complex in form, sometimes with interlocking patchworked panels in contrasting lamé fabrics, hexagonal panels embroidered and beaded with cobweb designs, or influenced by the fluid lines of antique kimonos. In the 1930s the bias cut that she had first used in the 1920s began to dominate; most of her gowns featured flared skirts and interesting seam arrangements and often incorporated scarves or ties that could be worn in different ways. She studied ancient Greek sculpture and produced fluid, draped gowns with cowl necks or crisscrossing ties.

Vionnet liked to use chiffons, gauzes (crêpe romaine, crêpe marocain), satins, lace, and velvets that, when cut on the cross, increased the stretch, but were also light and easy to wear and helped clothes to accentuate body lines and drape softly. She preferred solid-coloured textiles because prints, she felt, would lead the eye away from the shape and construction, which, for her, were the essence of the garment. For adornment, she preferred beadwork, cutwork, draping, fringes, faggoting (pulled and drawn threadwork), or appliqué. She often introduced textures into her work and, in particular, the rose motif. These could be in cutwork or of picot-edged silk to match the dress – she used these from the early 1920s until the late 1930s, when her house closed with the outbreak of war.

The look

In contrast to the sinuous, sensuous lines of the previous decade, the 1940s brought severe boxy shapes, wide shoulders, short skirts, eccentric hats, and clumpy shoes. World War II (1939–45) literally reshaped the clothes people wore, with rationing and the UK Utility scheme regulating the price and quality of clothing. Clothes needed to be practical and comfortable as in America and Britain women assumed men's roles in the workplace – flying planes, building tanks, and ploughing fields. Practical trousers, pleated skirts, shirt-waister-style or soft loosely structured dresses gave essential ease of movement.

The focus shifted from the torso to the extremities, with elaborate permed and rolled hairstyles and quirky angular hats, exaggerated, padded shoulders, and ankle straps, wedges, and platform shoes. Close short-sleeved sweaters or blouses with pussycat bows were often worn with fitted jackets and flared pleated skirts that finished on or just below the knee. Bolero-style jackets were popular for evening and were worn over matching gowns. Swagger coats with fullness falling from the shoulders, swinging coats, and military-style trench coats were popular. Evening dresses became simpler, with circle skirts, high necks, and ruched or smocked detailing around the bosom and midriff. Hip peplums or skirts with one-sided drapery were popular in the second half of the 1940s.

Tweeds, flannels, gabardines, cotton, synthetic jersey, and rayon taffetas were the most commonly used fabrics. Vivid floral patterns, which could be printed or stencilled on a dark satin background were in vogue, as was the use of sequins and beads (which weren't rationed) to decorate dark-coloured crêpe evening gowns. Even buttons were rationed but nonetheless added interest, colour or novelty; pockets became a major feature on tailored jackets.

While 1946 saw more emphasis on the hips, waist, and rounded shoulders, it was not until Dior's New Look of 1947 that a fashion revolution took place and women were finally able to luxuriate in his romantic vision of ankle-length dresses, basque bodices, and wasp waists. Every hard, angular line was softened and every curve emphasized. In 1949

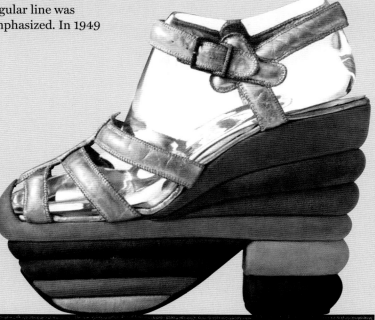

Below, Salvatore Ferragamo, rainbow-striped cork-soled platform shoes, 1938: these presaged the clumpy proportions of shoes made throughout the 1940s when platforms and wedges were popular. P

Introduction

THE AUSTERE & INNOVATIVE FORTIES

"Fashion is always of the time in which you live. It is not something standing alone." *Coco Chanel*

Right, Harper's Bazaar cover, November 1941: "Make do and mend" was a popular mantra as fabrics were channelled toward the war effort and became rationed for domestic use.

Right, Harper's Bazaar cover, November 1941: "Make do and mend" was a popular mantra as fabrics were channelled toward the war effort and became rationed for domestic use.

Left, Rita Hayworth in *You'll Never Get Rich* (1941): she wears a perky disc-shaped hat and matching scarlet dress with shoulder pads and draped, pleated crossover bodice – commonly found elements in forties dresses.

Below, In 1949 Hermès produced the "Eperon" handbag, which had rigid curved sides and was perfect for concealing black-market purchases. The brass clasp was inspired by the spurred heel (*éperon*) of a riding boot. N

a large number of garments became coupon-free, allowing women greater self-expression.

The rise of accessories

Accessories became increasingly important. Women wrapped their elaborately permed hair in scarves (often printed with patriotic messages) for ease of maintenance. Turbans were a major fashion feature and Schiaparelli produced some extremely elegant couture versions. Hats and furs were deemed non-essential to the war effort so hoods, skullcaps, snoods, hand-knitted berets, high-crowned straw boaters adorned with veils and ribbons, and disc-shaped hats (tilted over the forehead and held in place by a headband) proliferated. Fox-fur stoles with glittering glass eyes and pendant claws added a dash of glamour. With the shortage of leather, gloves were made from fabric, and handbags tended to be useful clutches or angular styles with looped handles.

Heels became higher, and in the early 1940s deeply unpopular wooden soles were introduced to eke out leather supplies. When the fashion photographer Cecil Beaton visited Paris after its liberation in 1944 he described the "heavy sandal-clogs which gave the wearers an added six inches in height but an ungainly, plodding walk".

Right, Six Lucie Rie glazed porcelain buttons, *c.*1940: buttons were a relatively cheap and quick way of cheering up an old dress, but in Britain rationing ruled a maximum of only four buttons could be used for new garments. F

THE EFFECT OF WAR ON FASHIONS IN EUROPE

Above, Wartime fashions with coordinated accessories and sensible low-heeled shoes, *c.*1944.

Below, Utility clothing label – "CC41" (Controlled Commodity symbol, 1941) – which showed the garment complied with government rationing controls. "CC41" Utility marked blue and white leaf-print gown. B

Below right and far right, Tweed Utility overcoat, mid-1940s, labelled "CC41", with velvet collar. C. "Free France" printed silk scarf by Jacqmar, 1940s, printed with patriotic messages from General de Gaulle. B

In Britain leading designers such as Digby Morton, Hardy Amies, and Norman Hartnell designed smart, practical dresses, coats, suits, blouses, and shirts for mass-production at affordable prices. These clothes carry the label "CC41" (Controlled Commodity symbol, 1941) and are highly collectable today. Home-made and ready-to-wear 1940s clothes (regardless of where they were made) are extremely sturdy, good quality, and generally very affordable.

In war-torn Europe, the flickering images of Hollywood stars dressed in luxurious creations by Greer, Adrian, and Irene provided respite in austere times, while the government's "Make Do and Mend" campaign encouraged people to reuse and alter existing garments. Unfortunately, many beautiful 18th-century dresses were cannibalized during this period as attics were raided. Curtains were transformed into evening dresses and wedding dresses were sometimes made from parachute silk. Amusing films by the British Ministry of Trade showed how to turn a dinner suit into a snazzy day suit, pyjamas into a day dress, or an old top hat into a chic beribboned bonnet. Many men must have come home from the war to find little left in their wardrobes!

Occupied Paris

In Paris, Schiaparelli reacted to the outbreak of war with her "Cash & Carry" collection featuring large pockets for emergency valuables. With grim humour, her "camouflage dress" could be lengthened into a full-length evening gown at the pull of a ribbon – very useful when "one emerged from the subway at night to attend a formal dinner". But Schiaparelli, Molyneux, Mainbocher, and Worth all relocated following the German occupation in 1940.

Despite this exodus, some 60 couture houses remained in operation and Lucien Lelong, president of the Chambre Syndicale de la Couture, persuaded the Nazis to abandon their plans to relocate the industry to Berlin. Many rich customers still fled the city (replaced to a degree by the wives and girlfriends of Nazi officers and black-marketeers) and international trade became largely impossible. Thus haute couture from occupied Paris is incredibly rare and valuable. The Chambre Syndicale's 1946 "Théâtre de la Mode", a tour of 200 miniature dolls dressed in the latest haute couture (including designs by Lanvin, Lelong, and Balenciaga) aimed to tempt buyers back. However, they only really returned for the debut collection in 1947 of Lelong's former assistant, Christian Dior.

AMERICAN FASHION
IN THE FORTIES

In 1940 American *Vogue* commented: "Into every mind concerned with clothes, the question repeatedly arises, 'What will America do without Paris Fashion?'" The United States had a tradition for high-quality, mass-produced ready-to-wear, but relied heavily on Paris for sartorial direction. With the fall of France, American buyers turned to home-grown talent – handbags were produced by Koret, hats by Lily Dache, and superb costume jewellery by Miriam Haskell. Many collectable and influential designers made stylish ready-to-wear, but Charles James, Valentina, and Mainbocher (the last of whom had relocated to New York from Paris in 1940) produced European-quality haute couture.

The use of separates – cardigans teamed with skirts or trousers, and peasant blouses with blue jeans – increased and Rita Hayworth and Lana Turner became "sweater-girl" pin-ups to the troops. The backless, crisp cotton Californian sundress formed part of the American look, while tailored suits had long jackets with exaggerated shoulders, narrow waists, and slim kick-pleat skirts. Classic evening gowns were typically columnar with side slits, in draped Grecian-style jersey or rayon faille, and ornamented with lavish beadwork or sequins.

Accessible style

The San Francisco company Lilli Ann (established by Adolph Schuman in 1934) also used British fabrics for added cachet. Unless extraordinary, Lilli Ann day suits are generally moderately priced, but some of the clever cutting with bands of colour moving from shoulder to hem or decorative detailing appeal to modern designers, so these can sell at a premium.

Sophie Gimbel (1898–1981) stocked French couture and copies at Saks Fifth Avenue but began designing herself as French supplies depleted. Her successful, sophisticated eveningwear (bearing the labels "Sophie of Saks" or "Sophie Originals") is as wearable today as when first made. A national favourite, but not internationally known, her gowns are moderately priced and mainly bought by a buy-to-wear clientele rather than collectors.

The stores of fashion entrepreneur Hattie Carnegie (established 1909) sold clothes, furs, accessories, jewellery, and even chocolate. Her incredibly successful business employed Norman Norell, Claire McCardell, Jean Louis, James Galanos, and Pauline Trigère, although their input was never acknowledged on the labels. Due to the volume produced, they are relatively inexpensive pieces, even with their good design and outstanding quality.

The wearable, sporty designs created by Claire McCardell (1905–58) typically incorporate spaghetti straps or ties at the waist, metal hooks in place of buttons, natural shoulders, and full dirndl skirts. Her early 1940s pieces with brass hooks are very desirable and can be expensive, but her later production is still relatively cheap.

Nettie Rosenstein (1890–1980) and Ceil Chapman (1912–79) produced fabulous and affordable ready-to-wear. Rosenstein's little black dresses were worn by woman all over the country and Chapman made well-designed evening gowns in rayon or synthetic mixes with sequins, beads, ruching, or pleats. Chapman's 1930s couture business was a financial flop but her 1940s ready-to-wear clothes (combining inexpensive fabric with excellent design) have become extremely collectable in recent years.

Fashion and Hollywood

The famed MGM costume designer Edith Head (1897–1981) relished the challenge of making glamorous outfits within the US's War Production Board's L85 regulations, and many successful designers started their careers in the big Hollywood studios. Los

"But this year, the needles of Paris have been suspended, temporarily we hope, by the fortunes of war. And for the first time in memory, an autumn mode is born without the direct inspiration of Paris. For the first time, the fashion centre of the world is here – in America."
American Vogue, 1 September 1940

Angeles designer Howard Greer (1896–1974) – who opened a couture establishment in 1927 and a wholesale business in 1930 – specialized in cocktail-wear and dinner gowns with elaborately decorated necklines and shoulders – reasoning that it was these parts that were most noticeable when a woman was seated at a dinner table. As Greer is not an internationally acclaimed designer, his impressive ready-to-wear gowns are still affordable.

The costume designer Gilbert Adrian (1903–59), who opened his Beverley Hills boutique in 1942, was also noted for elaborate cocktail-wear and lavish red-carpet gowns. He was credited with the American "Utility" suit with its interesting piping, tabbed detailing, and novelty pockets. He famously quipped of the New Look: "To try and make women pad their hips in this day and age is a little like selling armour to a man." Today, while his suits are fairly plentiful, his glamorous eveningwear is less so. Irene Lentz (1900–1962), Adrian's successor at MGM, established Irene Inc. in 1947, which supplied 25 department stores with extremely stylish day suits using British worsteds as well as dramatic, glamorous eveningwear. Cinema-goers were thus able to dress like their film idols at affordable prices.

Charles James

Mercurial in temperament, English-born Charles James (1906–78) was undisputedly the greatest American designer of the 20th century, so acknowledged for his cutting skills Dior is reputed to have said his creations inspired the New Look. However, he was a notoriously slow worker and spent most of his later years in litigation or fighting piracy of his designs.

An innovator, James cared little for mainstream fashion, spending years honing individual designs with mathematical precision and devising templates with interchangeable components for every section of a garment. Masterpieces included the ribbon dress and cape, the spiral zip on his famous "taxi" dress, and the "cloverleaf" gown (see page 79). His complex, sculptural ball gowns often feature asymmetric drapery.

While not a household name, James is undoubtedly one of the great couturiers. His brilliance and mastery of construction means no prestigious fashion collection should be without his work. Although some of his English designs from the 1930s have surfaced in Britain, he was more prolific in America where he had many wealthy (and patient) patrons in the 1940s and 1950s. But his erratic working practices make his work rare and hotly contested anywhere.

Below left to right, Howard Greer deep purple crêpe dinner dress, mid-1940s, labelled "Custom Original". D. Ceil Chapman gold satin evening gown, late 1940s, multiple satin buttons to the front, swag to front thigh, and trained hem. D

Below, Rare Charles James copper taffeta bias-cut gown with asymmetric skirt, 1940s. P

Right, Joan Crawford – in the film *Humoresque* (1946) – wears a Gilbert Adrian crêpe evening ensemble with exaggerated padded shoulders that serve to emphasize the narrowness of the jewelled waistline and slim hips.

Lauren Bacall (born 1924) was the perfect style icon for the 1940s. Unlike the simpering heroines that made up the bulk of her Hollywood contemporaries, she had a powerful screen presence that made her the equal of her "leading man".

Originally a model, Bacall was so terrified during her first screen test that to stop her face from quivering she lowered her chin to her chest and looked upward into the camera. This became known as "The Look". Aged just 19, in 1944 she starred alongside the veteran actor Humphrey Bogart in *To Have or Have Not*. Bacall's voice was trained to be lower and sexier, and Nancy Hawk, the wife of film director Howard Hawk, guided her in matters of manners, taste, and dress. Romance blossomed with the 45-year-old (and already married) Bogart and the couple wed in 1945. For the ceremony she chose a simple pink wool suit with a narrow leather belt instead of a traditional bridal gown. With her large catlike eyes and beautiful face framed by gently waved blonde hair, she still looked great!

Her classic look was understated chic – almost business-like elegance by day and sultry siren by night. Her wardrobe consisted of simple classics – crisp white shirt teamed with a broad leather belt and slacks or ankle-length skirt, or a well-tailored checked tweed suit with wide shoulders and slim waist. Her accessories always harmonized with the ensemble, rather than screaming for attention, and a cigarette was never very far from her coral-coloured lips.

Style Icon

LAUREN BACALL

"Stardom isn't a profession; it's an accident." *Lauren Bacall*

Left, Lauren Bacall in *To Have or Have Not* (1944), during the filming of which, not surprisingly, she caught the eye of her future husband, Humphrey Bogart. The bare midriff became a popular look in the mid 1940s.

Right and below, Bacall in 1947. Rare women's grey flannel trousers with coordinating blouse: probably because they were considered "ordinary", very few of these women's trousers have survived and are eagerly sought after by 1940s collectors. C

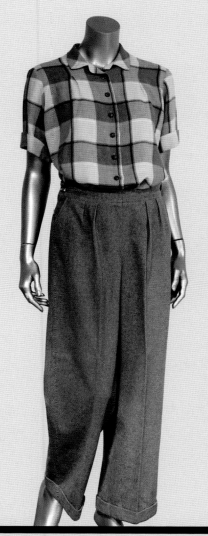

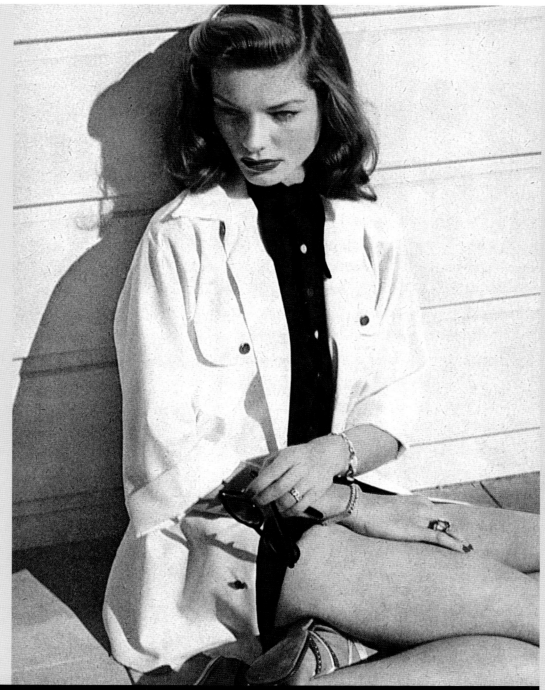

What would Lauren wear?

*Simple sweater or white blouse teamed with slacks or an ankle-length skirt *Espadrilles *Well-tailored, slightly masculine suits, accessorized with a charm bracelet or well-chosen brooch *Slinky satin goddess-style gown

In February 1947, against a backdrop of bomb-damaged buildings, rationing, and austere "masculine" fashions, Christian Dior's (1905–57) romantic vision burst upon the world with his debut "Corolle" collection. With "clothes for flower-like women with rounded shoulders, full feminine busts and hand-span waists above enormous spreading skirts", the collection celebrated the female form. Boned corsets – some with extra frills added to the hips and bra – made the angular forties look redundant overnight. The voluminous, ballerina-length skirts were further enhanced by layers of tulle, while cambric interlining was added to jackets to produce the desired rounded hips. Not since the 19th century had the female form been so distorted by corsetry and crinolines.

American *Vogue*'s Bettina Ballard reported, "We were witnesses to a revolution in fashion" while *Harper's Bazaar*'s editor-in-chief Carmel Snow is said to have exclaimed, "It's such a New Look", thereby giving the innovative style its name. Many deemed the copious amounts of fabric used to be unpatriotic, however. Moral arguments raged, but women the world over loved it and those who couldn't afford Dior took jackets in at the waist and added bands of fabric to their skirts, to emulate the look. Copies proliferated and Deréta, a British firm that had previously mass-produced Utility suits, now made grey-flannel New Look suits that sold out within weeks.

An enduring revolution

Although Dior changed silhouettes with each collection, he never entirely dismissed the New Look. It defined the following decade and was universally adopted by other designers and manufacturers. This collection reaffirmed Paris as the undisputed leader of haute couture and catapulted Dior (whose original staff of 85 rose to 1200 by 1955) into the forefront of international fashion.

Left, Wallis Simpson's black silk ensemble, *c.*1949–50: the lightly boned bodice with tulle inner corset and two interchangeable skirts. The Duchess remained a loyal customer of Dior into her old age. S

CHRISTIAN DIOR – THE SAVIOUR OF FRENCH HAUTE COUTURE

Pre-1952 clothes carry labels without dates, which are slightly smaller than the later examples and are sewn down in a pointed rather than square-ended fashion. However, coats and jackets from later ensembles were also often undated – so not everything with an undated label is necessarily early. The fabrics in the late 1940s are sometimes heavy and the finishing not as good as in the following decade; also, not all of Dior's ensembles have integral corsets. Great care must be taken when examining an early dress to ensure that it is correct; what may at first seem slightly on the crude side might, in fact, be the real thing. The debut collection is very scarce – were an original couture example of the "Bar" ensemble to come onto the auction market, so many museums have it on their wish lists that it would probably make six figures.

MADAME GRÈS – THE SCULPTRESS OF FABRIC

"Madame Grès" (Germaine Émilie Krebs; 1903–93) was one of the greatest couturiers of the 20th century. From the bias cut, through the New Look and the miniskirt, to the shoulder-padded excesses of the 1980s, with her masterful use of drape and cut, she is regarded by many as a sculptor in fabric. She reputedly trained with the Parisian couture house Prémet in 1930 before working for the couturier Julie Barton and changing her name to Alix Barton. "Alix" models featured in *Vogue* as early as 1933 and she may have established her own house, Alix Couture, in 1934. Some historians suggest that she was such a competent designer that Julie Barton renamed the existing company after her assistant.

From her 1937 marriage she became Madame Grès, and in 1942 opened her own house on the rue de la Paix. Forced to close for defying German fabric restrictions, after massive lobbying by members of the couture establishment she reopened in summer 1944, with a defiant display of red, white, and blue.

Madame Grès's clients included Wallis Simpson, Princess Salimah Aga Khan, and Jacqueline Kennedy but she shunned the Paris social scene. Working in solitude, she draped, cut, and tacked her carefully selected fabrics directly onto the figure, believing that the fabrics themselves would direct her.

Alongside Vionnet and Balenciaga, Alix Grès is a genius of construction. Her designs are complex, masterly, elegant, and hand-finished. The complicated Grecian draped gowns were her most famous "look", alongside ethnic-inspired gowns (including the one-shouldered sari) and tailored ensembles that incorporated exaggerated peplums, clever shoulder pleats, or integral drawstring fastenings. The construction is often surprising; while it was the tradition for couture houses to fasten dresses down the left, Grès frequently defied this rule.

No self-respecting fashion museum should be without a "signature" Grecian-style gown, though the draped jersey daywear tends to fetch less than the full-length evening examples. Alix-labelled examples are rare and amongst the most desirable couture. Her Grès-labelled pieces from the 1940s to 1980s are reasonably plentiful.

Opposite left to right, Rare, early gold and ivory silk damask evening gown, Winter, 1935, with 1930s "Alix" label. P. Fine bicolour draped jersey cocktail dress, c.1945. M. Example of 1940s "Grès" label.

Above, Madame Grès revisited her Grecian-style gowns throughout her career, with this version appearing in *Vogue* in the 1950s.

After the austerity and rationing of the war years came a desire for opulence, lavishness, and luxury. As men returned from the war, many women relinquished their jobs and swapped their sensible uniforms for aprons. As the need for practical, comfortable work clothes diminished, a yearning for the luxuries women had been denied for the last decade increased. In 1947 Christian Dior tantalized women with his extravagant creations – not since the 19th century had clothing been so restrictive, with boned, corseted bodices, wasp waists, and voluminous skirts. Rounded hips, accentuated busts, and ballerina-length skirts, as instigated by Dior's New Look, prevailed throughout the 1950s.

Toward the end of the decade, more relaxed silhouettes were championed by the young Yves Saint Laurent at Dior and by Givenchy and Balenciaga. By 1957 the waist-less, straight sack-dress had segued into the more fitted sheath silhouette with raised waistlines and, later, into the loose "baby-doll". However, even some of the most casual-looking clothes still relied on a hidden armoury of corsetry, girdles and suspenders. The "beat" look, with black polo neck and slacks, was adopted by the younger generation as the decade faded, while jeans and biker jackets became the uniform of young men influenced by James Dean and Elvis Presley.

In Paris, with its long tradition of grand fashion houses, skilled *petites mains* (the in-house seamstresses) were supported by specialist suppliers of silk flowers, embroidery, ribbons, millinery, lace, and buttons, while luxurious fabrics were often specially adapted to suit the taste of a particular designer. The houses themselves had strict hierarchies, with the couturier at the top and a director below who oversaw two principal ateliers, one dedicated to *flou* (dressmaking) and the other to *tailleur* (tailoring), each with their *premières* and *secondes*, specialist pattern cutters, *modelistes* (design assistants), seamstresses, *vendeuses* (handpicked saleswomen), and mannequins (live models).

This combination of excellence in design and execution led to some of the most dramatic, romantic, and superb couture creations of all time. Nothing was too complicated, too difficult, too labour intensive for the Paris houses. The words "haute couture" and "alta moda" in the 1950s meant a level of excellence that can only be dreamed of in modern times.

The creators

Although Christian Dior spearheaded the assault on ugly austerity, he was abetted by other major Paris-based designers including Jacques Fath, Jean Dessès, Cristóbal Balenciaga, Hubert de Givenchy, Robert Piguet, and Pierre Balmain. These designers are famed for their fabulous, romantic creations, which are among the most collectable and desirable of this period.

Across the Channel, Queen Elizabeth's marriage and coronation elevated the prestige of Norman Hartnell and of British couturiers in general – Hardy Amies, John Cavanagh, Digby Morton, Bianca Mosca, and Victor Stiebel, among them.

In Rome, in 1952, the Fontana sisters made the gown for Audrey Hepburn's cancelled wedding to James Hansen, and dressed stars such as Ava Gardner and Sophia Loren. Other highly collectable Italian designers are

Below, Hermès oxblood leather *sac mallette*, 1950s: the upper section is a handbag, but the hinged base has a concealed velvet-lined jewellery compartment, perfect for taking with you on a plane. F

THE LUXURIOUS FIFTIES

"A golden age seemed to have come again... What did the weight of my sumptuous materials, my heavy velvets and brocades, matter?"
Christian Dior

Right, The young Yves Saint Laurent surrounded by his mannequins posing in his Spring/Summer 1958 "Trapeze" collection, his first collection as chief designer at Dior. Note the new shape with volume falling from the shoulders to hem alongside the more traditional dress with bell-shaped skirts.

Simonetta and Fabiani, Roberto Capucci, and Antonio Castillo (who first collaborated with Lanvin before moving to Elizabeth Arden in the United States).

Postwar America, too, produced its own crop of highly successful designers including Charles James, Mainbocher, James Galanos, Arnold Scaasi, and Bob Bugnand. New York became a centre for well-made, mass-produced ready-to-wear, as generally accepted sizing standards were adopted across the country. Designers such as Ceil Chapman, Traina-Norell, Nettie Rosenstein, and Pauline Trigère produced affordable, wearable pieces, which are highly collectable, yet accessible, today.

Slick, ladylike perfection

Women were required to be pencil thin, corseted, coiffured, and perfectly accessorized with matching gloves, hats, bag, and shoes. Felt circle skirts, Mexican printed skirts, and cardigans with embroidered or jewelled details gave a youthful, more casual feel. Formal day suits had bracelet-length sleeves to show off the long gloves with complex creases at the wrists. Gloves in soft kid leather or satin were worn in the evening with a strapless sheath; the latter have survived in large numbers and, unless made by Dior or Hermès, are of relatively little value.

Costume jewellery completed the look and the brooch became a major feature. Rhinestone-studded, swirling gilt-metal styles, large gem-set flowers, and novelty animal shapes abounded. Brooches were worn on formal daywear as well eveningwear. Christian Dior produced high-quality accessories to complement the clothing lines and these are very collectable today. The pieces (many of which were manufactured in Germany) often carry the date of manufacture on the back as well as the signature. Other collectable names to look out for are Miriam Haskell, Coppola e Toppo, and Roger Scemama, as well as – to a lesser degree – Gustavo Trifari, Eisenberg & Sons, and Coro.

Hats ranged from small toques (worn over a slick chignon) to wide-brimmed picture hats. By the end of the 1950s hats became tall and conical and were often flower covered. Those by the major Paris houses and by Bes-Ben in the United States are highly coveted, but unlabelled or lesser labelled pieces are some of the cheapest collectables around.

Shoes were mainly high-heeled stiletto styles, with pointed or chisel toes. In Paris, Roger Vivier (who produced shoes to match Dior's couture creations) invented the comma heel and pagoda toe. His shoes are high quality, often bejewelled, and highly desirable.

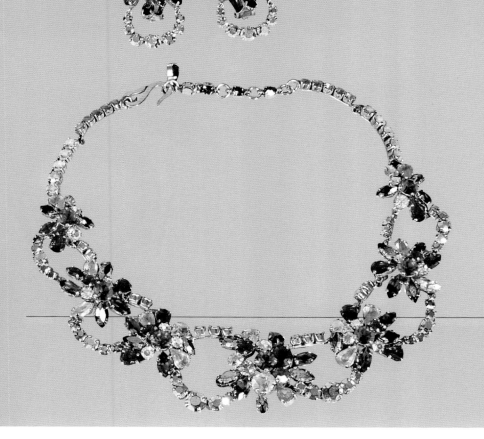

The couture gowns of Pierre Balmain (1914–82) are admired for their sumptuous materials, superb finishing, and luxurious glamour. His creations were romantic and ladylike, following the prevailing silhouettes and styles of the day. The owner of a Balmain gown could be confident that it would be impressive and opulent, but never vulgar. The designer commented:

> Sometimes I regret that my character does not drive me to create an occasional horror, for I believe that the nightmare of certain models can confirm the purity of lines. But I cannot force myself to do it.

Balmain's love of embroidery and appliqué is evident in the grand ball gowns of the 1950s and early 1960s – they are masterpieces of breathtaking complexity and skill. He would often conceal an opening or a vertical seam by fastening an appliquéd flower head to continue the floral pattern.

Balmain started as an apprentice to British-born designer Captain Edward Molyneux in 1936, where he remained until Molyneux closed his house at the outbreak of war. He was a major influence on the young designer.

In 1941 Balmain joined the grand couturier Lucien Lelong in occupied Paris where he worked alongside the young Christian Dior. They became good friends and spent many hours discussing plans to open a fashion house together. A few months after the liberation of Paris, Balmain set up his own house on rue François-1er. He opened the doors of his salon to rapturous praise in October 1945. Dior left Lelong to set up his own house in the spring of 1947 and, although Balmain believed that the decision to go their separate ways had been mutual, Dior felt betrayed and the two were hardly ever to speak or meet again.

Left, A fabulous ball gown, Autumn/Winter 1955/56, of ivory satin, embroidered with three-dimensional bunches of violets using velvet and silk ribbons, and studded with emerald and amethyst pastes. It has a matching pale violet satin voluminous coat. V

Right and below, Pleated chiffon ball gown with basket-weave effect skirt, 1953. Embroidered black satin cocktail gown, Autumn/Winter 1959/60: the satin by Leonard, the rococo embroidery by Lesage. J

PIERRE BALMAIN

"If a seam is not quite right, that is a matter of life and death."
Ginette Spanier, Balmain's directrice

Regal, lavish, and show-stopping

Pierre Balmain was every inch the couturier – handsome, well groomed, elegant, and skilled at handling the Parisian *grandes dames*. His clientele included royalty, statesmen's wives, and film stars; Queen Sirikit of Thailand made him her exclusive couturier.

It is only latterly that Balmain's importance has been fully recognized. Whereas in the past it was possible to purchase a wonderful Balmain piece for relatively small sums, his lavish ball gowns can now sell for the five-figure sums that they so richly deserve. However, the simpler cocktail-wear and daywear are still relatively accessible.

Although his heyday was the 1950s to early 1960s, he designed into the 1970s and upon his death the house was officially taken over by his assistant of more than 30 years, Erik Mortenson. In the 1970s the focus of the company turned to ready-to-wear, although couture collections were still produced. The gowns produced from the 1970s onward, when Balmain's personal input was reduced, are consequently of less value.

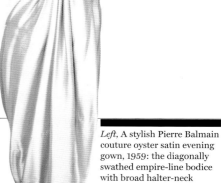

Left, A stylish Pierre Balmain couture oyster satin evening gown, 1959: the diagonally swathed empire-line bodice with broad halter-neck straps; hobble skirt. M

CRISTÓBAL BALENCIAGA – THE MASTER

A highly skilled pattern cutter and tailor, Cristóbal Balenciaga (1895–1972) intuitively knew how to achieve results through clever construction, using minimum darts and seams. He was universally admired – Christian Dior described him as "The master of us all" and Coco Chanel enthused, "Only he is capable of cutting material, assembling a creation and sewing it by hand. The others are simply fashion designers."

Balenciaga secured a tailor's apprenticeship in San Sebastián at the age of 12, establishing his first couture salon there in 1919. Five years later he registered his own company, Eisa B.E., taking large orders from the Spanish royal family. Further couture ventures followed in Madrid and Barcelona in 1933 (both temporarily closed in 1935). He established Maison Balenciaga, avenue George V, Paris in 1937. He quickly developed an international clientele and was one of the few foreign couturiers to remain in wartime Paris.

Balenciaga was reserved and detested the press (in 1956 he and Givenchy controversially showed their collections a week after the official Fashion Week to avoid its usual media circus, and continued to do so until Autumn/Winter 1967). He disliked interaction with his

"When I met Balenciaga, I realised I knew nothing about couture. In one of his ensembles, with just a single seam in the middle of the back, the line was so pure, so clear, that it conveyed simplicity in its very perfection."
Hubert de Givenchy

clients over business (prefering to mix with them socially) and, wearing his clinical white coat, he meticulously crafted his collections behind the scenes as the *vendeuses* took responsibility for selling the models.

Influences and signature style

Many of Balenciaga's creations bear testament to the culture of his native Spain. Diana Vreeland wrote, "His inspiration came from the bullrings, the flamenco dancers, the fishermen in their boots and loose blouses, the glories of the church, and the cool of the cloisters and monasteries. He took their colours, their cuts, then festooned them to his own taste." Sometimes black on black, his pieces create wonderful textures using faceted jet beads, droplets, velvet, and corded bands. Elaborate black passmenterie was sometimes contrasted with the pale blue or yellow reminiscent of matador costumes, while tiered, flamenco-like skirts, strong colour contrasts, and layers of mantilla-like black lace adorned evening gowns.

The influence of Dior's New Look is evident in the nipped-in waists, pronounced curves, full skirts, or long, tight pencil skirts of Balenciaga's early 1950s dresses and suits. His massive, voluminous tent coats of Ottoman silks or luscious velvets became a signature style, highlighting his fascination with proportions. Triangular godets inserted at the underarms to give more freedom of movement are also typical and he used the minimum number of seams, often cutting the fronts of

a coat in one piece with the front of a sleeve. With Balenciaga, less was always more.

For day, he designed comfortable, wearable clothes with clever cutting rather than restrictive corsetry, including thousands of wearable little tweed suits which are still relatively easy to find today. His day dresses and cocktail-wear could be in a solid pastel silk or a large-scale dramatic print with outsized checks or massive flower heads. These simple dresses often belie the mastery of their construction with clever wrap-around, draped sack-backed bodices and concealed fastenings. For day and evening he often showed a layered look, such as the "zócalo", a tunic-like overdress worn over an underskirt, the hem with a matching or contrasting fabric. For evening he selected solid colours, such as pale blue, sapphire, lilac, ivory, shocking and salmon pinks, apple greens, and, of course, black, to create drama and draw the eye to the gown's architectural shape.

Textures were added in the form of elaborate beaded or sequined bodices or trims, or layers of overlaid lace. A simple pastel-coloured sheath would be worn underneath an elaborate organza coat or jacket entirely covered with brightly coloured ostrich strands or silk blossoms. The embroidery specialist Lesage also produced specially commissioned, elaborate fabrics, embroidered to shape in floss silks, rich textured chenille, or in imitation of the flowers found on Spanish shawls. In the late 1950s and early 1960s Balenciaga also liked to use bold chiné floral taffetas for evening gowns and coats.

Below left, One of the designer's best clients, Ava Gardner, models a striking poppy red linen suit with matching hat, 1952.

Below, Voluminous black silk faille tent coat, *c.*1958. These enormous, cape-like collars (which can be lifted over the head to form a hood) were used by Balenciaga from 1948 right through the 1960s. M. The "Eisa" label was used on couture made in Balenciaga's Spanish houses.

Below, Ivory gazar gown, Spring/Summer 1967: note the sculptural streamlined shape, devoid of adornments. Balenciaga made this as a wedding gown with conical gazar hood-like veil. M

Below right and far right, Couture embroidered ivory shantung cocktail gown, Spring/Summer 1960: princess line with graduated waist, bell-shaped skirt, the Lesage embroidery reminiscent of embroidery found on Spanish, or "Manila", shawls. M. Paris couture label.

With Balenciaga, it is always the construction of the gown that we should notice first. The more streamlined, sculptural and apparently simple it appears, the better. As the 1950s progressed, Balenciaga grew ever more confident and masterful in his own style in which simplicity was key. His major innovations of the 1950s were the middy line of 1951 (where the focus shifts from the waist to the hip), tunic line (zócola) of 1955, the sack or chemise of 1957 (both styles with no waists at all), the empire line of 1958 (waistline raised to below the bust), and the baby-doll of the same year with a solid-coloured, fitted sheath worn below a cascading lace overdress or silk taffeta dress with flounced hem.

Balenciaga's last collection was Spring/Summer 1968. He abhorred the vulgar excesses of the new decade. In a rare interview he stated: "The life which supported couture is finished. Real couture is a luxury which is just impossible to do anymore."

Market

Spanish-inspired pieces from the 1940s and 1950s are highly sought after because they demonstrate Balenciaga's faithfulness to his own heritage combined with his clever construction and use of colour and texture. Pieces which follow the prevailing early-fifties trends are generally less sought after than the freer, more radical designs of the late 1950s and 1960s – the more dramatic, more sculptural, and more architectural the piece, the higher the value. The myriad little tweed day suits he made throughout his career are plentiful and still relatively affordable.

The "Balenciaga, avenue George V" labels are haute couture from the Paris house and those with "Eisa" labels are haute couture from his Spanish salons. The finish and fabrics tend to be of a slightly higher quality in the Paris house, but both are haute couture.

BALENCIAGA
10, AVENUE GEORGE V. PARIS

"Grace" was the perfect name for this innately elegant, serene woman (1929–82). When she embarked on an acting career, her style was conservative American ready-to-wear, she would turn up to auditions in prim business-like suits teamed with crisp white gloves and hat. Laura Clark, editor at *Harper's Bazaar*, described her look as "almost schoolgirlish."

Her blossoming Hollywood career and her meeting, in 1954, the suave French-born American fashion designer Oleg Cassini (1913–2006), changed all this and they planned to marry. This was not to be but she was frequently photographed wearing his collection. Her casual look was Capri pants, plain cotton shirt, headscarf, and espadrilles. She was the original twinset-and-pearls girl.

She was admired as much for her on-screen style as for her acting. In *To Catch a Thief*, with costumes designed by the legendary Edith Head, she wore stylish beachwear with winged sunglasses and hair concealed beneath a scarf and hat, and for evening an ethereal Grecian-style gown in floating white chiffon redolent of designs by the Parisian couturier Jean Dessès. She collected her Best Actress Academy Award in an Edith Head-designed ice-blue satin gown sculpted to emphasize her slender waist and complement her blue eyes and blonde hair, with small bow, matching spaghetti straps, and trained, cascading rear skirt. Kelly often wore shades of blue, pastel pinks, beige, pure white, and her favourite colour – yellow.

In 1955 Prince Rainier of Monaco proposed and she tied with Babe Paley at the top of the US Best Dressed List (interesting as Mrs Paley dressed entirely in haute couture while Kelly at this point hardly ever did). For her wedding gowns, Kelly turned to MGM's Helen Rose, wearing a fitted suit of rose taffeta overlaid with beige guipure and ballerina-length full skirt for the civil ceremony and a spectacular dress with fitted Brussels lace bodice, wide cummerbund sash over bell-shaped faille skirt and full train for the church. Her trousseau of 40 outfits made up a "who's who" of American designers and fashion houses including James Galanos, Ceil Chapman, Traina-Norell, Harvey Berin, Pauline Trigère, Adele Simpson, Mollie Parnis, Larry Aldrich, Christian Dior – New York, Ben Zuckerman, Suzy Perette, and Claire McCardell.

As Princess Grace of Monaco, she patronized the Parisian couture houses, including Yves Saint Laurent, Lanvin Castillo, Grès, and Chanel, though her favourites were Dior, Balenciaga, and Givenchy. However, it is an accessory that has become synonymous with the star. What we have come to know as the Hermès "Kelly bag" was actually patented by the company in 1935, as the *Sac à dépêche*. It was renamed in honour of the princess in 1956, because she was constantly photographed carrying the bag to disguise her pregnancy. The finely crafted Kelly bag remains an icon of quiet good taste – rather like the princess herself.

Below, Kelly on the set of *To Catch a Thief* (1955). Hermès Kelly bag, 1950s. <u>K</u>

Right, Kelly wearing a Dessès-style draped chiffon evening gown, but designed by Edith Head for *To Catch a Thief*.

Style Icon

GRACE KELLY

"I think it is important to see the person first and the clothes afterwards." *Grace Kelly*

Christian Dior caused a worldwide sensation when he showed his first collection in February 1947 and dominated Parisian haute couture and the fashion world at large until his untimely death. Throughout the 1950s the world watched to see how short or long his hemlines were and the shapes and directions of each new collection.

In sharp contrast to his handsome, suave contemporaries, Dior was shy, middle-aged, balding, and overweight. But his creative vision and drive were on fashion rather than on himself. The infrastructure of a Dior gown is almost architectural and he famously said "without foundation there is no fashion". His ball gowns required no underpinnings, everything was incorporated – the integral corsets had special stretch tulle grounds while skirts came with layers of stiffened tulle, often edged in horsehair or nylon at the hems, diaphanous upper layers of organza with silk being worn next to the skin. Some even came with suspenders for the stockings. The shapes he created were sensuous, voluptuous, and incredibly feminine.

Dior would work up a basic pencil sketch, followed by a calico toile when hundreds of tiny adjustments were made. The correct accessories and jewellery for the ensembles were meticulously selected then he would price up each outfit – taking into account the cost of the fabric and time each took to make.

Trafalgars

Dior christened each of his twice-yearly collections (a tradition for many designers to this day), inspired by a mood or a favourite flower, or the silhouettes of the clothes themselves. The key pieces that illustrated the main direction or silhouette of that particular season were called his "Trafalgars", which the fashion press awaited with bated breath. However, he maintained mainstream designs to simultaneously please the press and ensure his collections were a financial success.

Dior the businessman

By 1950 Maison Christian Dior accounted for 50 percent of the entire export profit of French couture and his shows attracted all the major US department store buyers, for whom the import duty on his dresses was prohibitively expensive. Alternatively copies could be made (under strict licence) of individual gowns by the department store's own dressmakers; if the original couture dress was then re-exported into Canada the original duty paid could be reclaimed. It's therefore not unusual to find superb haute couture in Canada!

Another option was for the store to purchase the toile (the actual pattern) with agreement to make a strictly controlled number of gowns domestically, avoiding import duty altogether. These licensed copies carry "Patron Original" labels. The quality and fabrics can vary and they are not true haute couture pieces but the designs are still superb.

Dior for all

In 1955 Dior opened his first boutique for the middle and lower ends of the market, selling trinkets, scarves, and other accessories as well as the clothes themselves. The boutique-labelled gowns can still have couture finishes, especially if the client was an important one. They were "semi-couture" and the dress could have one fitting or alteration if necessary.

These pieces were also available at 87 overseas Dior licensed studios. The important studios (such as New York or London)

Below, Flame-red, taffeta evening gown with organza-lined fitted bodice and matching orientalist pantaloons (not pictured). This is from Autumn/Winter 1958/59, Yves Saint Laurent's first year as the house's head designer. U

Right and bottom, Dior fits a dress to his model, c.1950. Pale blue satin shoes with matching satin roses, 1950s, made by Roger Vivier who produced innovative and stylish shoes for Dior from 1953 to 1963, using fabrics that exactly matched the couture gowns. Note the curve in the heel – Vivier's most famous invention was the comma-shaped heel. B

DIOR IN THE FIFTIES

commissioned couture pieces for clients overseen by the studios' head designers (Marc Bohan in London). However, their staple was the official Dior ready-to-wear pieces with house labels such as "Dior London" or "Dior New York" (but no collection dates). These used good quality fabrics, correct Dior corsetry, and the great Dior patterns (adapted for mass-production) but with ready-to-wear machine finishes internally. Sold in standard sizes, only minor alterations were allowed.

Dior was the first haute couture house to become a truly global super-brand; royalty-based licences were also granted for making furs, jewellery, stockings, and ties, without Maison Dior's involvement in the manufacture. It was thereby possible for a woman to purchase a pair of stockings or a perfume and feel touched by Dior luxury and magic – something that was very close to Dior's own heart.

Dior was also astute in recognizing that he was an ageing couturier and that fresh, young blood was needed in order for the brand to continue to dominate and succeed. In 1955 the "King of Couture" chose as his dauphin the young Yves Saint Laurent – a case of one genius recognizing another.

The king is dead. Long live the king!

When Dior died in October 1957, France went into mourning and his protégé, the young Yves Saint Laurent (1936–2008), who had collaborated with Dior on his last collections introduced his first Dior collection in January 1958. It was a massive hit with loose-fitting, younger, more streamlined clothes (though inside, rigid boning and corsetry invisibly held the body in place). Less fussy or opulent, and with a triangular silhouette with fabric falling from narrow shoulders to a wide hemline, he still included some bejewelled ball gowns typical of the mid-century lines, to please more orthodox clients and the house's continued success was ensured.

Collecting Dior

In the 1990s it was possible to purchase a sublime haute couture embroidered and beaded cocktail dress for as little as a few hundred pounds or dollars. The same dress today could command five figures as the market has escalated and interest in Dior in particular has grown. Dior is a jewel in the vintage fashion crown. His clothes embody the romance of the period, combined with the highest possible levels of couture finishing, fabrics, and design.

All the Maison Dior creations from the 1940s and 1950s are desirable while those of the fledgling young Saint Laurent of 1958–9 are also particularly sought after. Just a few years ago "Dior London" and "Dior New York" labelled pieces could be purchased for relatively low sums, but, as prices for the haute couture pieces escalate, these, too, are now hotly contested. With these diffusion lines you get true Dior design and construction, but with cheaper fabrics and ready-to-wear finishes.

Top to bottom, "Patron Original" label – an original Dior design but not made in the Dior house. Christian Dior haute couture label with date. Dated labels were used from 1952 onward. Christian Dior ready-to-wear label from the late 1950s: similar labels appear for the New York fashion house.

"I moulded my dresses to the curves of the female body, so they called attention to its shape." *Christian Dior*

Left to right, "Avril", a crisp white organza gown embroidered with bunches of violets, Spring/Summer 1955. R. Dior London brocaded pink satin evening gown, *c.* 1958, with empire-line bodice, obi-like belt with detachable bow, full tulip-shaped skirt and tulle petticoats. L. A fine Christian Dior haute couture brown tulle "Esther" evening gown, Autumn/Winter 1952. U.

Chanel's creations are timeless classics and vintage couture pieces are as wearable today as when they were made. Combining comfort with minimalism and seemingly effortless style, anyone purchasing a Chanel suit can be confident in the quality and longevity of the ensemble. Generations can wear the same Chanel suit and feel equally empowered by it.

In 1953 the 71-year-old Coco Chanel came out of retirement, annoyed and dismayed by the corseted, constrained silhouettes produced by Messieurs Dior, Fath, and their ilk. She launched her new collection on 5 February 1954 to mixed reviews. The European fashion press were initially hostile; they had not forgotten or forgiven her for literally sleeping with the enemy in Occupied Paris. However, the American response was rapturous and the influential journalist Bettina Ballard championed her. Chanel had produced smart, wearable, and, most importantly, comfortable clothes that the more athletically minded US buyer could relate to – stylish navy wool suits with contrasting crisp white collars and cuffs, jackets punctuated by silk organza camellias, drop-waisted dresses redolent of the 1920s (at a time when women's waists were cinched to extreme levels), and romantic lace cocktail dresses. Chanel loved lace and since the 1920s she had produced layered, tiered lace gowns in pastel tones and severe black. The mid-1950s incarnations were romantic, feminine, full-skirted dance gowns, which did have structured boned bodices to produce the correct silhouette. For eveningwear, women were required to suffer just a little!

Since the 1920s she had played with knitwear, jersey, and tweeds, but in the 1950s the Chanel suit was to come into its own as a signature style and status symbol. Princess Grace of Monaco was photographed wearing one at Christmas with her children; Romy

Left to right, Wine and ivory satin, and spotted organza cocktail gown. L. Couture lace evening dress with fitted bodice and ruffled hemline. M

Right, Coco Chanel fitting a tiered tulle cocktail dress with brooch at the waist in 1959.

POSTWAR CHANEL

Schneider wore them on screen and off, and Elizabeth Taylor had examples in gold brocatelle lined in contrasting raspberry silk.

Effortless elegance

The Chanel suit of the 1950s and 1960s didn't change dramatically. Uniquely, they could be worn from day into evening. The suits from both decades had contrasting braid trims, pocket details, and chain-weighted hems that ensured that the jacket was held in place correctly. In the 1950s the skirt was longer and slimmer, while in the 1960s it became more A-line and the hem gradually rose. The couture suits usually came with a simple silk camisole-like bodice, or a blouse with detachable cuffs complete with cufflinks, in a matching fabric. The jackets are quilted for added comfort and the linings relate to the colour of the blouse. Chanel took enormous care over the construction of the sleeves and how they were inserted, preferring a higher-set armhole and narrow sleeves. She went to endless pains to ensure that they were absolutely perfect, demanding that her seamstresses unpick them repeatedly until she was satisfied: "A skirt is made for crossing the legs and an armhole for crossing the arms."

The 2.55

To complement her clothes, Chanel designed and commissioned luxurious accessories. In February 1955 she produced an updated version of her handbag – of quilted jersey or leather with chain shoulder strap. This was the birth of the classic 2.55, available in black, navy, and dark brown with wine grosgrain or leather linings. Black-tipped two-tone leather shoes with sling-backs were also introduced in the 1950s and are reminiscent of the correspondent shoes she had worn herself in the 1920s; these were another important component of Chanel's signature style.

Chanel also commissioned jewellery redolent of the magnificent pieces she herself had been wearing since the 1930s – ropes of pearls, gem-inset bangles, poured glass camellia brooches, earrings, Maltese cross pendants, and long glass and pearl sautoirs, made by Robert Goossens and Gripoix. The fake jewellery was always priced to be expensive, making it even more desirable!

Chanel vintage is extremely collectable, be it the clothes or the accessories. Couture from the 1960s is contested by museums and buy-to-wear clients and so, though affordable, the prices can climb on occasion. Boutique pieces from the 1980s onward are mainly bought to wear because the vintage prices are a fraction of the cost of a new shop-bought boutique example and so provide excellent value for money. Leather 2.55 bags (and, to a slightly lesser degree, the jersey examples) are design classics and many women feel their wardrobes are incomplete without at least one! Chanel's timeless, exquisite costume jewellery is much sought after, and the pieces made by Gripoix in the 1930s can fetch four figures.

Top to bottom, 1960s "Chanel" couture label. 1980s "Chanel boutique" label.

Left, Black resin cuff, stamped "Chanel" with pearl and green and red glass. L

Below, Couture lilac and black tweed suit, Autumn/Winter 1959/60. G

Right, Couture beige tweed and navy satin suit, *c.*1957: lion's mask buttons, chain weighted, lined in navy silk, knee-length skirt. G

In 1960 young men and women dressed like their parents in semi-corseted dresses, coordinating accessories and respectable suits with ties. But the decade that followed was a period of seismic change with London at its epicentre. Space travel, Pop art, retro looks – from Edwardian dandies to thirties gangsters' molls – and the hippy movement were all major influences on the decade. Collars and ties were discarded in favour of rollnecks, collar-less Beatle jackets, velvet jackets, and frilly shirts. Non-shrinkable, drip-dryable synthetic fibres with bright colours were embraced by haute couture houses as well as by retail clothing stores.

Youthful rebellion

The new fashions showed the postwar spirit of youthful rebellion with liberation for men as well as for women. This was the decade of the "dandy" with British *Vogue* featuring young men dressed in Edwardian vintage fashions salvaged from family attics or Portobello Road. Celebrities such as The Beatles and The Rolling Stones embraced collar-less suits, lavish military uniforms, floral shirts, Indian beads, and kaftans. The use of recreational drugs, the widespread adoption of the Pill, and greater social mobility than ever before, helped to create the "swinging sixties".

It was also an age of innocence, when the pre-war strictures of the Establishment were rejected in favour of "peace and love", and this was reflected in the clothes. Jean Shrimpton and Twiggy modelled the clothes produced by Ossie Clark, Marion Foale, Sally Tuffin, and Zandra Rhodes, all youthful, innovative alumni of London art colleges, and everyone clamoured for "the London Look". Hairstyles got progressively bigger, often by using added hairpieces or wigs, and in 1963 Vidal Sassoon introduced the geometric bob to complete the "dollybird" look.

In 1964, predating Yves Saint Laurent's version by two years, Marion Foale and Sally Tuffin produced the highly controversial female trouser suit. It was a symbol of liberation but women wearing them were frequently refused entry to restaurants and the *Daily Mail* noted "Girls Will Be Boys. Like it or not – and many men don't." London fashion was leading the way and Paris, so used to being in the vanguard, could not ignore the surge of innovative talent coming to light in the British capital. Slowly but surely the Paris *maisons de couture* adopted many London ideas, expanded them and took them to another level. The only couturier to completely reject the miniskirt was the great Cristóbal Balenciaga. He found the whole thing too vulgar and retired in 1968.

The rarefied world of Parisian haute couture was already shaken by the young Yves Saint Laurent whose last collection for Dior in 1960 was highly controversial and a financial flop but also hugely influential. *Vogue* reported: "The beat look is the news at Dior ... pale zombie faces; leather suits and coats; knitted caps and high turtleneck collars, black endlessly." His collection was

Introduction

THE REVOLUTIONARY SIXTIES

"The sixties were so different from the fifties, the colours, the drugs, the freedom." *Jean Shrimpton, fashion model*

too radical for his clientele and in 1961 Marc Bohan, whose timelessly elegant, ladylike suits and eveningwear received rapturous reviews, replaced him.

Elsewhere the United States had elected a youthful, dynamic president, John F Kennedy, whose glamorous wife wore classic Givenchy-inspired suits and dresses in solid, often pastel colours by Oleg Cassini and Pauline Trigère. Despite the ongoing Cold War, there was a feeling of optimism and a preoccupation with everything futuristic; the space race gripped the public imagination. Paco Rabanne, André Courrèges, and Pierre Cardin produced futuristic ensembles incorporating plastic, vinyl, and metal, and Andy Warhol's *Campbell's Soup Cans* was reproduced on disposable paper dresses.

By the close of the decade there were several fashion strands all in play at the same time – you could be a romantic Edwardian-style heroine dressed by Gina Fratini with ruffles and ringlets; a hippy-chick in a Thea Porter kaftan with flowers woven into your wavy Pre-Raphaelite locks; wear ethnic prints and embroidered Afghan coats with love beads and headbands; or go psychedelic with Emilio Pucci. The Mod look had segued into hippy, bras were being burned, and Ossie Clark and Yves Saint Laurent were producing sheer, transparent, figure-hugging clothes designed to emphasize the naked breasts. This was the time of the Summer of Love, the student revolution in Paris, anti-Vietnam War demonstrations, and an increasing interest in Eastern philosophies and communal living. Love and peace, man!

Above, Model in floral minidress by Pauline Trigère, photographed in the suitably exotic Shiv Niwas Palace, Udaipur, Rajasthan, in 1967.

Right, A Paco Rabanne metal tunic with matching visored helmet, 1966.

MARY QUANT

Above, Mary Quant with her signature cropped Vidal Sassoon haircut, surrounded by models wearing her innovative injection-moulded plastic bootees, 1967.

Above, Mary Quant make-up crayons in tin, late 1960s A. "Mary Quant" woven label. *Below,* A pair of Mary Quant injection-moulded plastic bootees, mid-1960s: daisy logos to the heels, with plastic straps, eyelets and buckles to the upper edge; lined in stockinette, which shows through the clear plastic upper. C

The boutique movement began with Goldsmiths graduate Mary Quant (born 1934), who opened Bazaar on the King's Road in 1955. Expensive in comparison to other shops, the simple shapes, Peter Pan or frilled collars, and below-the-knee hems appear relatively uncontroversial today. But the look was youthful – simple day dresses of orange wools, striped tweed effects, and towelling. Quant used her ever-changing avant-garde shop windows to attract media coverage and, with her Vidal Sassoon geometric bob and wearing her own designs, she created a signature look that thousands were to imitate.

In 1962 Quant created the cheaper "Ginger Group" – mass-produced ready-to-wear clothes that were distributed to boutiques and department stores nationally. In the early 1960s the US chain store J. C. Penney purchased 6000 garments, and in 1965 she made a fortune as a result of the "Youthquake" trip, a clever marketing exercise devised by Karl Rosen, president of the ironically named Puritan Dress Company, and J. C. Penney's Paul Young. Its aim was to introduce America to swinging British fashions and Quant's contemporary, Sally Tuffin, recalls being met with hostility because her everyday clothes of short dress and boots were deemed unseemly at best and indecent at worst. Accompanied by British models including Pattie Boyd, a red London bus, and an American Beatles sound-alike group called The Skunks, Quant took 30 of her outfits on a whistle-stop tour of 12 cities in 14 days. In 1966, she accepted her OBE in a minidress. Although not the "inventor" of the minidress, she certainly popularized it and made it an international look.

Market

Although cutting edge when they were made, Quant's early pieces – which are often in unusual colours such as burnt orange, brown, or tweeds – look quite sober to modern eyes and can fetch modest sums at auction. The later pieces incorporating plastic or vinyl are more typically "swinging sixties" and often command higher sums. Value rises if a dress can be cross-referenced with a photograph of the piece being modelled in the period, because museums then become more interested. Ginger Group mass-produced pieces and the myriad accessories Quant made are all collectable but relatively inexpensive.

Right and far right, Ginger Group linen minidress, mid-1960s. B. Black and white wool day dress, 1963. Jean Shrimpton modelled this in *The Sunday Times*. It originally cost 25 guineas. L

By 1967, 15- to 19-year-olds were buying about half of all the womenswear being sold in the UK. They shopped on Saturday and in the evening wore their purchases, dancing to the latest hits in a discotheque, another innovation of the period. Cathy McGowan of the TV pop programme *Ready Steady Go!* was an influential role model – what she wore on a Friday night would be purchased in huge numbers the following day.

Customers were no longer content to wait months for the next season's look and the small boutiques, with their young designers, were able to react quickly to incorporate the latest fashion nuances, which helped to tempt shoppers back with new material. The boutiques could sell out on a daily basis and were often restocked with fresh merchandise overnight. The shops themselves, such as Granny Takes a Trip with its dark cavern-like interior and a bumper car seemingly crashed through the store window, were enticing; loud pop music played and staff were often indistinguishable from customers. In 1962 Marion Foale and Sally Tuffin opened their first shop just off Carnaby Street. Taking the lead from Mary Quant, they both manufactured the clothes and retailed them. Jean Muir for Jane & Jane likewise set up and ran a highly successful business, while Sylvia Ayton and Zandra Rhodes, backed by the actress Vanessa Redgrave, set up the Fulham Road Clothes Shop. One of the most innovative figures was John Bates, who, with no formal training, designed often ground-breaking ranges (Marit Allen of *Vogue* credited him with the invention of the miniskirt) that could be sold via department stores, both under his own name and also "Jean Varon" because customers continued to react favourably to a French-sounding name.

In London, Biba and Mr Freedom turned their shops into "lifestyle" stores where you could buy not only clothes but also furniture and even food. Biba opened its doors in 1964 and reached a massive audience through mail-order catalogues. Chain stores such as Dorothy Perkins and Wallis produced well-designed, affordable "gear" for the masses, with Wallis making a fast-selling copy of the traditional Chanel suit. Menswear boutiques were concentrated on London's Carnaby Street, King's Road, and Savile Row, where clothing by John Stephen (the "King of Carnaby Street"), Mr. Fish, Lord John, Tommy Nutter, Blades, Top Gear, Countdown, and I Was Lord Kitchener's Valet drew in the capital's youthful peacocks. Surprisingly, however, menswear of the flamboyant dandy type from this period is hard to find and highly sought after, so perhaps there weren't so many male "cool cats" as the press of the time seemed to suggest.

Celebrities also got in on the act – the footballer George Best set up his unisex boutique in Manchester in 1967 and Cathy McGowan and Twiggy followed suit. There was a proliferation of boutiques across Europe and the US, and in 1963 Sonia Rykiel designed a range (that Brigitte Bardot was regularly seen wearing) for the Paris boutique Laura.

Youthquake

In July 1965 the first "Youthquake" trip officially brought the miniskirt to America. The trips continued in following years with British designers and models such as John Bates and Jean Shrimpton being introduced and featured in US *Vogue*. Instead of garments being imported, with all the resultant shipping costs and import duties, British designs were mass-produced by J. C. Penney, which often brought the retail price as low as $20–30 a garment.

Up to 3000 people would turn up to these much-hyped fashion show experiences and, buoyed by their success, Paul Young opened the first Paraphernalia boutique in New York in 1966, selling British and European fashion

Below, Fulham Road Clothes Shop printed yellow satin trouser suit, late 1960s, labelled "Zandra Rhodes and Sylvia Ayton". F

Right, Three models in dresses by Betsey Johnson for Paraphernalia and opaque tights by Solar.

THE BOUTIQUE MOVEMENT

Left, Mr. Fish royal blue velvet man's jacket, late 1970s: orange "Clifford Sreet" label; lined in blue and white printed foulard silk. E

Below, "John Stephen Carnaby St"-labelled red damask satin double-breasted jacket, late 1960s. John Stephen was hailed as the "King of Carnaby Street". In 1967 he said: "Carnaby is my creation, I feel about it the same way Michelangelo felt about the beautiful statues he created." L

Mr.Fish
17 CLIFFORD STREET
LONDON, W.I.
PHONE 734-9311
MADE PECULIARLY FOR
38

THIS GARMENT SHOULD BE DRY CLEANED

Below, Two colourful silk
minidresses, mid-1960s.
Each A

and also work by young innovative American designers such as Betsey Johnson. The actress Susannah York opened the shop – an inspired choice as she had just starred in a film about young groovy designers called *Kaleidoscope*. Clever marketing, combined with cutting-edge fashions and mass-produced affordable designs meant that by 1968 there were 44 Paraphernalia franchises in the US.

Back in Europe, Yves Saint Laurent, realizing the decline of haute couture, opened his first Rive Gauche store in 1966. It was the first time that a great couturier had given as much thought to ready-to-wear as to haute couture. Lanvin, Givenchy, Nina Ricci, and Pierre Cardin quickly followed suit.

Mass-produced boutique clothing, when not linked to a specific famous designer, is very affordable. As a rule, if it was cheap to buy when it was new, it is cheap to collect today (although a notable exception is flamboyant menswear, which commands high prices at auction). Mainstream chains and brands such as Dollyrocker, Ginger Group, Sambo, and Bus Stop produced great designs but in cheaper fabrics and finishes. Colourful mass-produced polyester minidresses, which encapsulate the sixties look, are some of the cheapest collectables of all. These tend to be purchased by the buy-to-wear market rather than by niche collectors because they are fun, affordable, and easy to wear.

It all began with a haircut. Leonard, the fashionable Mayfair hairdresser, chose a 16-year-old schoolgirl, dyed her hair, and cut it close to the scalp in a sleek, short, boyish crop when big bouffant, back-combed hairstyles or long hair with fringes were the prevailing looks of the day. Deirdre McSharry, fashion editor at the *Daily Express*, liked the hairstyle but loved the model more, and requested an interview with her, declaring Twiggy (born Lesley Hornby, 1949) "The Face of 1966".

Despite her youth, Twiggy possessed poise and presence in front of the lens. Photographers adored her. Diana Vreeland of US *Vogue* declared her, "the mini-girl in the mini-era" and within a year she had appeared in 13 separate *Vogue* fashion shoots and appeared on the cover internationally five times.

In February 1967 she launched "Twiggy Dresses", designed in collaboration with Paul Babb and Pamela Proctor, two young recent Royal College of Art graduates. The dresses, retailing at £6 to £13, were simple, colourful, and easy to wear – "switched-on without being gimmicky", as Twiggy told the *Sydney Morning Herald*. Each piece came with a free Twiggy hanger carrying a portrait of her face and the label ran successfully for three years.

The range also launched in America where she was met with a frenzy of press photographers at the airport and ABC television produced a series of three documentaries recording her visit. The label reputedly received more than a million dollars of orders before she had even left New York, however cheap pirated copies flooded the market before her company had a chance to respond. In Japan in 1968, she was fêted, photographed, and mobbed by fans. Twiggy dresses, although highly collectable, are still relatively accessible price-wise.

Twiggy retired from modelling after just four years declaring, "You can't be a clothes hanger for your entire life!" Despite this short career, her effect was profound. Her slender, adolescent physique and long, slim legs (hence her childhood nickname of "Twigs") were perfectly suited to the prevailing fashions of the time – whether androgynous trouser suits, simple A-line little-girl dresses with pretty collars, or futuristic, geometric shapes with minimal decoration. She was the first supermodel to achieve global superstar status and her hauntingly beautiful, innocent face became the iconic, definitive look of the 1960s.

Below left to right, A Twiggy dress hanger, *c.*1967, used in the Twiggy boutique and given away free with every dress sold. A. Yellow organdie Twiggy dress, 1967. D

Right, Twiggy, photographed by Gösta Peterson for *The New York Times*, 1967. Twiggy Dresses reputedly received more than a million dollars worth of orders before the model even left New York after launching her label stateside.

Style Icon

TWIGGY

"The Cockney kid with a face to launch a thousand shapes."
Daily Express, 23 February 1966

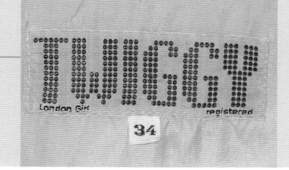

What would Twiggy wear? *Little-girl-style minidress with matching patterned or glittery tights to emphasize her slim legs *Low-heeled shoes of metallic leather or with large buckles *Dangly plastic earrings *Three pairs of false eyelashes plus painted-in eyelashes and eyeliner

In 1964 the French designer André Courrèges (born 1923), an expert tailor who had served an apprenticeship under Balenciaga, fused Givenchy's and Balenciaga's clean lines and geometric shapes with space-inspired vinyl trims in the "moon girl" look. Dominated by white and silver, glittery tights, metallic leather shoes, massive chrome necklaces, clear plastic bangles, and bauble earrings completed the look. Courrèges teamed skirts with blunt-toed, calf-length boots; he produced suits with massive hoods, accompanied by white plastic sunglasses with slits and visors; dresses and trouser suits were dense but supple, made from top-stitched wool jersey; and angular cowgirl hats were teamed with striped lime and cream jersey dresses and jackets.

By 1966 Pierre Cardin (born 1922) had also joined the fashion space race and would continue the look into the 1970s. Jackets with massive quilted circle collars, hems cut with lobed circle panels, and black wool dresses with massive chrome ring or necklace collars are typical. Bodices were cut away to reveal the waist and emphasize the neck and shoulders. In 1966 Cardin produced a radical man's suit – a zip-fastened tunic top worn over a rollneck sweater with knickerbockers and boots.

In London meanwhile, John Bates (born 1938) produced a radical wedding ensemble for *Vogue*'s "Young Ideas". This featured a minidress and matching coat made of white gabardine trimmed with silvered PVC, with a matching silver PVC flying helmet. Lurex and brocatelle were also used heavily in 1966 – all the major Paris houses chose these shimmering fabrics for cocktail-wear.

Plastic sculpture

British *Vogue* declared: "Suddenly everyone is talking about Paco Rabanne and his plastic sculpture." Rabanne's (born 1934) pieces, which used plastic, vinyl, silver, and fluorescent coloured leather, are often described as works of art. However, he is most renowned for his chainmail tunics, such as the silver disc minidress Audrey Hepburn wore for *Two for the Road*, where platelets made of silver metal or plastic linked by chains were worn over flesh-coloured body stockings and tights (see page 101).

These tunics were not for the faint-hearted – avant-garde and expensive they undoubtedly were; comfortable they were not. In consequence, sixties examples are rare and command high prices at auction. In the 1990s Rabanne produced, as a magazine collaboration, a small Perspex bag containing plastic discs, metal hooks, and pliers – everything you needed to make your own kit-dress. These are often made up and sold as the sixties original – so be warned!

THE SPACE AGE COMES TO FASHION

Above left to right, Courrèges white leather moon boots, *c.*1967: zip and Velcro fastened, with original box. J. Rare André Courrèges couture futuristic ball gown, 1968: of white jersey, lined in white cotton. Q

Below, Pierre Cardin cream wool crêpe "circle" jacket and minidress ensemble, *c.*1969: labelled "Pierre Cardin Paris Collection Modèles Exclusifs pour l'Allemagne"; the jacket collar and hem formed from a quilted circle. M

PIERRE CARDIN
PARIS ·
"COLLECTION"
MODÈLES EXCLUSIFS POUR L'ALLEMAGNE

In 1965 the simple geometric Mod look prevailed. Shift dresses, jackets, and coats became contrasting experiments in black and white, reflecting a fascination with the effects found in Bridget Riley and Victor Vasarely's Op art. Made from paper or plastic as well as traditional fabrics, it was an idea with which all the major designers played. On graduating from college, Ossie Clark was featured with his black and white suit in *Vogue*'s "Young Ideas" pages. James Wedge's boutique Top Gear used the Mod emblem of a black and white target on jewellery and carrier bags, and it was also adopted by The Who as their logo.

The most famous, iconic, and desirable of all art-influenced creations came from Yves Saint Laurent's Winter collection of 1965 – the "Mondrian" cocktail dresses in wool or heavy silk crêpe, with blocks of primary colours within a grid of black lines. The sharp, clean lines of the collection made a huge impact and cheap imitations flooded the market in Europe and the US. The following year Saint Laurent brought out his "Pop Art" collection, which again used blocks of colour in simple but bold designs – using the dress as an artist uses a canvas. While the couture originals are extremely sought after and command huge sums at auction, the cheap retail imitations are still relatively affordable.

Paper dresses

Something of a sixties phenomenon, started by the Scott Paper Company as a marketing gimmick, the "Paper Caper" dresses were made of reinforced paper and came in a black and white Riley-style and a red and yellow print with paisley motifs. They sold in their thousands and sparked a proliferation of imitations and variations – from paper wedding dresses, underwear, and bikinis, to a paper dress stencilled with the letters NIXON in red for the presidential campaign of 1968. In Britain in 1967 Harry Gordon launched "The Poster Dress". They were in black and white newsprint and comprised variously a spaceship, a cat, a rose, Bob Dylan, Audrey Hepburn's eye (see page 96), and an Allen Ginsberg poem – the rarest and most valuable of these are Dylan and the spaceship, closely followed by the eye.

Inspired by Andy Warhol's iconic screenprint, the US soup manufacturer Campbell produced their "Souper" dress around 1966–7. This is one of the most expensive paper dresses to buy today as they appeal to modern art collectors as well as fashionistas. Yellow Pages or Op art dresses are more affordable as they are less visually dramatic and iconic.

POP AND OP ART INFLUENCES

Opposite, A group of paper dresses: Scott Paper "Paper Caper" Op art dress, *c*.1966, C; James Sterling Paper Fashions "Nelson Rockefeller" dress, 1960s, C; Mars of Asheville "Nixon" campaign dress, 1968, D; Mars of Asheville "Butterfinger" dress, *c*.1968, C; Mars of Asheville dress with hem printed with traffic-light spots. C

Below left to right, Marco Correa black and white Op art gown, late 1960s–early 1970s. F. Yves Saint Laurent couture "Mondrian" dress, Autumn/Winter 1965/66: of silk crêpe de Chine. This Mondrian gown is made even rarer because it is made of silk rather than the more commonly found wool. It is one of the most desirable and collectable dresses in the world. W

Right and above, Yves Saint Laurent black and white zigzag-striped Op art wool suit, *c*.1966. R. Bridget Riley, whose Op Art inspired fashion designers, in 1963.

HUBERT DE GIVENCHY

Hubert de Givenchy (born 1927) went to Paris in 1945 at the age of 17 intending to show his designs to "the master of them all" – Cristóbal Balenciaga. Unfortunately, he was turned away at the door by Balenciaga's stern *directrice*, Madame Renée d'Esling. Rather than return home empty-handed, he took his sketches to Jacques Fath, who hired him on the spot. The young Givenchy was to spend a year with this dynamic designer before moving to Robert Piguet for a year, Lucien Lelong for six months (the Lelong house closed in 1948), and then four years with the great Elsa Schiaparelli, eventually becoming responsible for the Schiaparelli boutique.

Having gained a wide range of experiences at these major houses, Givenchy opened his own establishment in February 1952. His first collection consisted mainly of separates and simple tailored suits, but they were fresh, young, and easy to wear with no contrived detailing. Some of the clothes were ready-made, some required just one fitting, while only a tiny number were strictly made to order as traditional couture outfits. Givenchy's debut collection was met with such adulation by the press and buyers alike that he decided to go the full haute couture route after all.

After years of wishing to meet his hero Balenciaga, they met in New York in 1953 where Balenciaga was signing a licensing agreement. Balenciaga became his friend and mentor and, although they never worked together, the older man passed on valuable advice to his protégé. They showed their collections at the same time and the freedom of movement and classic simple lines of their collections were often difficult to tell apart. However, although the end results could be very similar, their approaches to design were very different. Balenciaga – the master tailor – did a preliminary sketch, then a toile (a canvas pattern), followed by the selection of the fabric and the final dress. Givenchy, by contrast, always began with the fabric and worked closely with the major textile houses of the day. In 1968 when Balenciaga closed his house he advised his clients merely to cross the road and visit "Monsieur Givenchy".

Chic, understated style

Givenchy became synonymous with the chic, understated style of his most famous client and muse Audrey Hepburn (see pages 118–19), who declared in *Ciné Revue* (1962): "Everything I have worn for the last ten years has come from Givenchy, and I will probably remain faithful to him for the rest of my days. You may wonder why I attach such importance to Givenchy. It is because he creates quality clothes which combine simplicity and beauty."

When in the salon Givenchy always wore a white coat (as did Balenciaga). He sought perfection in every detail, always seeking purity in the line. Although his most famous couture creations were for his friend and muse Audrey Hepburn, the staple of all of the Paris houses at the time was the chic little day suit for wearing about town. Although his ball gowns and glamorous eveningwear can command high sums, classic couture suits and coats by this great designer are not uncommon and are still relatively affordable.

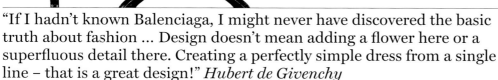

"If I hadn't known Balenciaga, I might never have discovered the basic truth about fashion ... Design doesn't mean adding a flower here or a superfluous detail there. Creating a perfectly simple dress from a single line – that is a great design!" *Hubert de Givenchy*

Far left and left, Couture wine velvet and black satin cocktail dress, *c.*1959–60: edged in bugle beads and spotted with faceted sequins. I. Couture cream silk evening gown with elaborately beaded and jewelled midriff, originally belonging to Audrey Hepburn, 1968. P

"To dress a woman is to make her beautiful."
Hubert de Givenchy

"The smell of silk is unique ... fabric is alive: I let the fabrics guide me and my imagination goes to work as soon as I have put them down."
Hubert de Givenchy, Geo magazine, September 1985

Audrey Hepburn (1929–93) was not just a film star; she was also a major style icon of the 20th century – our adoration of her luminous beauty, effortless elegance, and ladylike decorum only increases as the years go by.

Audrey had the slender, colt-like figure of a ballerina – indeed, she had trained as a dancer as a girl but was rejected on the grounds of her height. With a keen sense of her own unique style, Audrey knew what suited her. She preferred to wear pastel colours, black and ivory, with occasional hot pink thrown in for good measure, and believed that pale colours brought out her dark eyebrows and hair.

There was one designer to whom she turned throughout her life – Hubert de Givenchy (see pages 114–17). While, on first meeting, he was initially dismayed to encounter the then little-known Audrey rather than the legendary Katherine Hepburn, their collaboration on *Sabrina* meant the wardrobe received as much acclaim as Audrey's performance, and she later had it written into film contracts for him to make all the clothes that she wore for *Funny Face, Love in the Afternoon, Paris When it Sizzles, Charade, How to Steal a Million* and, most famously of all, *Breakfast at Tiffany's*.

Givenchy also made both of Audrey's wedding dresses – that of 1954 was of simple white organza and had a full skirt, demure high neck, and balloon sleeves, while the 1969 version was of pale pink mohair/cashmere with long sleeves and empire line with bow and matching headscarf. But arguably the most famous dress of all was the little black dress for *Breakfast at Tiffany's*.

Below left to right, Givenchy couture turquoise cloqué silk cocktail gown, Autumn/Winter 1966/67. Hepburn wore this dress to promote *Two for the Road* (1967). V. Givenchy couture shocking pink silk columnar crêpe sheath with asymmetric neckline, Autumn/Winter 1966/67. U. Givenchy couture black cloqué silk dress worn to promote *Paris When it Sizzles* (1962), the empire-line bodice cut high at the front and low at the back, with rear bow ties. U

Right, The most memorable of all Givenchy's dresses for Hepburn is the ultimate "little black dress" worn in the role of Holly Golightly in *Breakfast at Tiffany's* (1961). The black columnar gown with curved cut-aways, which frame the shoulder blades, is very simple, but devastatingly elegant. When a version of this dress made by Givenchy was sold at auction in 2006 it made £467,200 ($923,187), which reflects its importance.

Style Icon

AUDREY HEPBURN

"She knew exactly how she wanted to look or what worked best for her, yet she was never arrogant or demanding. She had an adorable sweetness that made you feel like a mother getting her ready for a prom."
Edith Head, Hollywood costume designer

What would Audrey wear?　*A silk sheath dress by Givenchy *Ballet pumps *A belted trench by Burberry *A crisp white shirt tied at the waist *A striped Breton top *Slim black pants *Big sunglasses

DESIGN IN AMERICA

The US provided real competition to the Paris houses at the more sophisticated, less avant-garde end of the fashion spectrum. Although the First Lady, Jackie Kennedy, adored French designers, especially Givenchy whose couture she wore for her 1961 Parisian visit, on US soil she patriotically consoled herself with designs by Oleg Cassini – whose pastel-toned ensembles with pared-down detailing, simple boxy jackets with self-covered or large single buttons, and pillbox hats were so reminiscent of Givenchy designs. The "Jackie Look", which was both youthful and sophisticated, was widely admired and imitated. Cassini's 1960s clothes rarely come up at auction, so perhaps their owners simply loved them too much to let them go.

French-born Pauline Trigère (1909–2002) was another designer who favoured less rather than more in terms of decoration. A favourite of Wallis Simpson as well as Jackie Kennedy, Trigère often used wool for cocktail and evening gowns – something that was considered unusual at the time – and she favoured pared-down, narrow silhouettes. She liked to play with trim details to create dramatic effects. Her 1960s capes in bold plaids or solid pastels were very successful and are just as wearable today. A master cutter and skilled tailor, she created clothes that were timeless and effortlessly sophisticated.

Bill Blass (1922–2002) became one of the most popular and well respected of America's designers in the 1960s. He adopted aspects of men's tailoring in his womenswear, in both his simple day clothes and his evening clothes, teaming sharp-lapelled blouses with silk trousers. His clothes weren't particularly radical and they were rarely showy – his preference was for wearable, elegant, and affordable pieces that used lace rather than sequins or beading and with skirts that rarely went higher than the knee.

By contrast, Norman Norell's (1900–1972) clothes were sumptuous and glamorous. Following the retirement of his partner Anthony Traina in 1960, he renamed their fashion house after himself. His clothes were expensive to buy, beautifully made, and often lavishly adorned. For Norell, more was more and he experimented with styles and decoration. A minidress could be covered in a shimmer of large, outsized sequins, and in 1961 he introduced a cut velvet culotte jumpsuit whose matching coat was trimmed with sable. During the 1960s he liked to play with the trouser ensemble for both day and evening – and for evening they were usually embellished with his beloved sequins.

Geoffrey Beene (1924–2004), sometimes described as "a designer's designer", set up his own company in 1963 after working for Teal Traina. In contrast to many of the creations of the 1960s, he steered clear of the avant-garde, preferring a youthful, almost schoolgirlish look of easy-to-wear short wool day dresses and little-girl high-waisted dresses, while for evening he created long relaxed jersey dinner dresses, short sequined evening dresses (sometimes with feather hems), and full-length ball gowns. He used the best fabrics and always had an eye for quality and detail.

Rudi Gernreich (1922–1985) was an Austrian-born but California-based designer. Trained as a dancer, his clothes always took into account the wearer's comfort and ease of movement. His trademark looks were graphic knitted or colour block patterned fabrics, often incorporating triangles, spots, or checks and strong, contrasting colours. He liked to play with transparent panels, cut-outs, nudity, transparency, and androgyny. He roundly declared in 1962 that "bosoms will be uncovered within five years", and two years later invented the topless swimsuit, which became an international sensation, denounced from pulpits the world over. Only around 3000 of the garments were sold, and so today they are highly desirable collector's pieces.

The *enfant terrible* of American fashion didn't stop there, inventing the seamless "No Bra Bra", that held the breast in place without radically altering the shape and stating in *Vogue* that, previously, bras had "been like something you wear on your head on New Year's Eve". This radical and fresh approach to fashion, with innovative designs, matching accessories to complete the "look", and affordable prices were further popularized by his friend and muse, the model Peggy Moffitt with her geometric haircut and pronounced eye make-up. Gernreich, a prophetic, original, and controversial designer, saw his clothes not only as something to wear but also as social statements. Although many of the knitted pieces produced in association with Harmon Knitwear are still relatively affordable, the more outrageous and iconic pieces are highly prized and hotly contested at auction.

In today's vintage market all these designers are accessible, with only the major, dramatic red-carpet gowns commanding high sums.

Left to right, Geoffrey Beene grey wool and rhinestone-trimmed evening gown, late 1960s. M. Norman Norell brocaded shocking pink satin evening gown, early 1960s. L. Sarmi yellow silk gown, early 1960s. D

Right, Rudi Gernreich's infamous topless swimsuit, *c.*1964: modelled by his muse, Peggy Moffitt.

By the end of the 1960s hemlines could be micro, maxi, or midi; transparent fabrics, cutaways, backless, topless had all been experimented with and there was, it seemed, nowhere else to go. The super-modern, urban chic minimalist look of the 1960s had begun to run out of steam and the hard, geometric lines of the Mod style began to give way to softer silhouettes. There was no single, major style dictating what people wore but different styles all running concurrently.

In Yves Saint Laurent's Africa-inspired Spring/Summer 1968 haute couture collection, he produced intricately latticed dresses formed from coloured glass and wooden beads, some with jewelled Maasai-like collars, as well as his iconic Safari suit. The chic, suburban woman could now appear as a huntress in the urban jungle and the Rive Gauche versions sold in large numbers. The African collection is one of the most valuable of YSL creations and even his complete Rive Gauche cotton Safari ensembles can sell for five-figure sums, they are surprisingly rare.

Real ethnic clothes – Indian prints, embroidered Afghan coats, love beads, hairbands – were the cheaper way to achieve the "back to nature" look. The Beatles led the way with their long hair, kaftans, and love beads, while at 1968's Woodstock people danced naked apart from garlands of flowers. Body awareness, the appreciation of the naked form, became another trend, with Ossie Clark

THE DECADE'S END

Above left to right, Pucci printed velvet bag, 1960s. E. Louis Féraud printed "hippy"-style jersey evening dress, c.1969–70: the front with green-faced Medusa-like figure. F

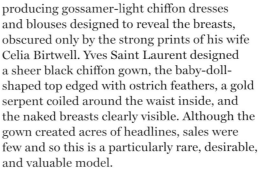
producing gossamer-light chiffon dresses and blouses designed to reveal the breasts, obscured only by the strong prints of his wife Celia Birtwell. Yves Saint Laurent designed a sheer black chiffon gown, the baby-doll-shaped top edged with ostrich feathers, a gold serpent coiled around the waist inside, and the naked breasts clearly visible. Although the gown created acres of headlines, sales were few and so this is a particularly rare, desirable, and valuable model.

Exotic kaftans were a wardrobe staple from 1967. Thea Porter (born 1927) produced transparent chiffon versions, patchworked with rich oriental brocades and edged in gold braid, and Elizabeth Taylor and Princess Margaret were devotees. The more colourful and diverse the fabrics in a Thea Porter kaftan, the greater the appeal and value today.

Psychedelic influences were strongly in evidence with Emilio Pucci (1914–1992) and the French fashion label Leonard as the main exponents. Swirling hallucinogenic patterns and reinterpretations of art nouveau designs (also fashionable in artwork, posters, and record sleeves) were printed onto fabrics in a kaleidoscope of vivid colours. Sixties Pucci examples appeal to both collectors and buy-to-wear clients, yet at auction an original sixties dress still costs a fraction of a brand-new example. Pucci printed silk jersey or velvet garments are more desirable than cotton or printed synthetic examples. Full-length dresses with plunging necklines combined with strong patterns and colours, avant-garde play-suits, and dramatic full-length evening capes command the highest prices.

The birth of vintage

The final "look" was the romantic, antique-style dress worn with ringlets and ribbons. Gina Fratini, Mexicana, and others pedalled pseudo-empire-line, pseudo-Edwardian dresses in white cotton, bedecked with frills from neck to hem. This retro look is one of the least expensive areas to collect and the value will probably not rise until the desire to wear frills becomes a major fashion trend again. Others chose to wear real vintage – Victorian bodices, beaded 1920s dresses, and lace inset Victorian gowns. This phenomenon was actually the birth of "vintage fashion".

Left and right, David Bowie in concert at Earls Court in 1973, wearing the androgynously styled Ziggy Stardust jumpsuit, designed by his friend Freddie Burretti. Hot pants teamed with David Bowie T-shirts and pageboy haircuts, 1973.

Introduction

THE RADICAL SEVENTIES

"We were all dressing a generation who were newly independent. They didn't have to ask their mother's opinion and they didn't want to wear their mother's clothes." *Barbara Hulanicki*

While some 1970s styles, including the Edwardian, ethnic, and retro art deco looks, carried through from the late sixties, this was a decade of radical change. Superbly crafted artisan clothes were produced by Bill Gibb, Zandra Rhodes, and Ossie Clark. Fashion could now also be art.

Away from these labour-intensive one-off creations, designer-labelled, ready-to-wear collections exploded, with Calvin Klein and Ralph Lauren building huge empires selling at premium prices. Haute couture saw its clientele shrink and was viewed as something of a loss leader, to help sales of diffusion lines, cosmetics, and perfumes. Saint Laurent's controversial 1971 forties-inspired collection was a financial flop, but his luxurious, exotic 1976 Russian collection silenced his detractors and reasserted his pre-eminence as the leader of French haute couture. Ungaro, Givenchy, Marc Bohan at Dior, Jules-François Crahay at Lanvin, Jean-Louis Scherrer, Capucci, Valentino, and Madame Grès continued to produce elegant haute couture models for their well-heeled international clientele.

On the street it was a different story. Separates came into their own and the trouser suit was commonplace, worn by all age groups, be it in corduroy or pastel-coloured Crimplene. A-line knee-length, midi, or maxi skirts, or wide flared trousers, were teamed with knitted tank tops, blouses with busy prints (sometimes worn with velvet chokers), printed cotton hats, and platform shoes or boots. Hot pants, often worn with coloured tights or teamed with a maxi coat, were popular. Skimpy halter-neck tops were worn with high-waisted trousers whose wide legs served to make the waist seem even smaller. Diane Keaton's Ralph Lauren-designed *Annie Hall* wardrobe was highly influential, with women wearing waistcoats, men's jackets, and even ties. Shirts and blouses often had long pointed or curved collars. Synthetic textiles were printed up in a range of styles – from designs inspired by art deco and Pop art to graphic, floral, and geometric patterns. Denim was the uniform of youth, the crotch-grabbing, high-waisted jeans often customized with embroidered novelty appliqués or patchwork. Gloria Vanderbilt became the queen of the "designer jean" in 1978 when her own range sold millions.

In London, street fashion continued to thrive. For evening you could be a Victorian heroine courtesy of Laura Ashley's printed cotton dresses or a 1930s *Bonnie and Clyde*-style Biba siren, or wear ethnic flower-child kaftans by Thea Porter or revealing floating chiffons by Ossie Clark and Celia Birtwell. You could wear metallic jackets, sequined bodices, velvet skirts, feather boas, floppy hats, and satin trousers and jackets from Biba, Granny Takes a Trip, Miss Mouse, or Mr Freedom, teamed with impossibly high Terry de Havilland metallic snakeskin platforms or boots glam-rock style, as epitomized by the androgynous David Bowie and pretty Marc Bolan. Antony Price, responsible for the super-cool tailored look of Bryan Ferry and Roxy Music, made bespoke suits for the men and curvaceous cocktail dresses for Jerry Hall. He launched his own label in 1979.

In New York, in 1976, Studio 54 opened its doors and welcomed in the likes of Bianca Jagger, Jack Nicholson, and Diana Ross. The disco look was born. Roy Halston's classically simple draped gowns, with bodices open to the waist, front, and back in richly coloured crêpe de Chine, satin, or sequins, were as at home in the night club as in the opera house. A glamorous, body-conscious new look – leggings with stilettos, skin-tight bandeau tops, Spandex and Lycra stretch dresses in fluorescent colours – was guaranteed to attract attention.

Left, Lionel Avery green leather "glam rock"-style men's platform boots, early 1970s: Avery's clients included Alice Cooper, Stevie Wonder, Slade, Suzie Quatro, and Gary Glitter. **F**

Back in London, there was "Anarchy in the UK" when Malcolm McLaren and Vivienne Westwood's defiant, anarchistic shops launched. The duo ushered in arguably the century's last major fashion movement and their punk designs reflected a Britain in the throes of economic downturn and mass unemployment, and whose disillusioned youth could see "no future".

Market

Any haute couture and some diffusion lines from the major French houses are of interest, while other collectable labels include Biba, Mr Freedom, Miss Mouse, Ossie Clark, Bill Gibb, Zandra Rhodes, Jean Muir, Janice Wainwright, Karl Lagerfeld at Chloé, Louis Féraud, Loris Azzaro, Yuki, Kenzo Takado's JAP, Kansai Yamamoto, Bus Stop, Sonia Rykiel, Courrèges, Cardin, Pucci, Leonard, Roy Halston, Geoffrey Beene, Norma Kamali, Giorgio di Sant' Angelo, and Rudi Gernreich.

Mass-produced designer daywear by mediocre brands of the 1970s is of very little interest to collectors or buy-to-wear clients. Brands with a significant identity such as Biba, Mr Freedom, and Granny Takes a Trip are the exception, but even these can be relatively cheap. Clothes from boutiques and chain stores such as Wallis, Dollyrocker, Bus Stop, and Mexicana are plentiful and inexpensive.

Below left to right, Thea Porter kaftan, early 1970s, composed of chiffon and exotic brocades. M. Loris Azzaro deep turquoise jersey dress and matching hooded cape (not pictured), *c.*1970: halter-neck collar and plastron of Coppola e Toppo floral beading and sequins in shades of blue and silver. J. Antony Price for Plaza metallic-blue lamé cocktail dress with wrapover fan-pleated bodice and skirt, 1979. C

Right, Bianca and Mick Jagger arriving at the Metropolitan Museum, New York, 1974. She wears a scarlet sequined Halston halter-neck dress with matching beret.

The brainchild of Barbara Hulanicki (born 1936) and her husband, Stephen Fitz-Simon, Biba was not just a shop, it was an experience. What began as a small clothing boutique in 1964 became a department store selling lifestyle products, cosmetics, shoes, hats, childrenswear, and menswear, as well as the bias-cut 1930s retro womenswear for which it was famous. The clothes weren't particularly well made and often of cheap fabrics, but they were well designed and the press coverage and glamorous in-store displays made them feel very special. Little dresses had high-set sleeves and armholes, curved collars and A-line skirts. Lace – sometimes in art nouveau patterns, similar to the scrolling design used on early labels – was popular, as were satin art deco-inspired eveningwear gowns that looked like 1930s lingerie. Accessories included wide felt hats in bright colours and cut with holes like a Gouda cheese, feather boas, platform shoes and boots, and glittery wellingtons.

Around 1974 Hulanicki introduced the angular 1940s shoulder-pad look. Tapestry coats with accentuated shoulders, angular, black faux-fur lapels, and large buttons were extremely stylish and appeal to collectors and museums alike. For the summer collections her unusual colour palette of mauve, purple, aubergine, brown, old rose, and grey was injected with pastel colours. Cosmetics were coloured to match. The clothes were affordable and accessible to the masses, in 1968–69 in mail-order catalogues with atmospheric photoshoots by the likes of Helmut Newton and Sarah Moon.

Biba lifestyle

In 1973 the Derry & Toms department store on Kensington High Street became the Biba flagship and included the Rainbow restaurant and a roof garden with pink flamingos. You could purchase Indian wicker chairs, peacock feathers, hat stands, and even specially branded dog food and baked beans. Stock vanished faster than it could be replenished, and large quantities were shoplifted. Biba finally closed in 1975. Tantalizing photographs of its stunning interiors ensure that it remains one of the most iconic and memorable of London's stores.

Although some of the more show-stopping lace evening gowns and faux-fur jackets can command high prices, the majority of Biba garments are moderately priced and the separates are especially inexpensive. It's a fun area in which to collect because you don't need to spend a fortune to put together a good collection and the range of Biba clothing, accessories, and merchandise is immense.

BIBA

Above left to right, Satin art deco label, *c.*1973–5, used on accessories. Striped satin ensemble, mid-1970s with printed art nouveau label. C. Leopard-print patent leather platforms. D

Top and right, Woven art nouveau "Biba" label, *c.*1969–71. Biba founder, Barbara Hulanicki, in the store with her husband, Stephen Fitz-Simon, *c.*1973.

Above, Yves Saint Laurent black crêpe "Le Smoking" ensemble accessorized with strings of pearls, hat, and cane, *Vogue*, 1973.

YVES SAINT LAURENT
IN THE SEVENTIES

Below, Yves Saint Laurent Rive Gauche "Lips" print dress, *c.*1971. I

Right, Haute couture ensemble from the Autumn/ Winter 1976 "Russian" collection. This was one of Yves Saint Laurent's most romantic offerings, fusing the exoticism and vibrant colours of Diaghilev's *Ballets Russes* with elements from North Africa, the Balkans, and the Orient. More affordable Rive Gauche versions included paisley- and floral-printed cotton skirts and quilted jackets. W

Yves Saint Laurent's 1971 "Liberation" collection disturbed some of his rich, conservative clients. The sexy collection had nothing to do with the austerity of war but was a reminder of the lavish wardrobes of "the horizontal collaborators". It engaged with the strong shift toward vintage looks seen in the bias-cut clothes produced by Ossie Clark and Biba. However, to put 1940s-inspired clothes – with their wide shoulders, knee-length skirts, turbans, and platform shoes – onto the haute couture catwalk was a brave move, and *The New York Times* described it as the "ugliest show in town". "Liberation" was a commercial flop and in consequence is highly desirable because it's quite difficult to find. The Rive Gauche version was more widely embraced by younger, trendier women. Today this collection is seen as visionary, canonical, and ground-breaking.

Having introduced "Le Smoking" dinner suit in 1966, Saint Laurent continued his pioneering use of trousers. Although radical at the time of its introduction, the dinner suit became a staple in fashionable women's wardrobes in the 1970s. This sexy, androgynous look – the formal structure of the male tuxedo contrasting with feminine blouses – was a great success and Saint Laurent began producing beautifully tailored versions for daywear. Although Marlene Dietrich, Greta Garbo, and Katherine Hepburn were photographed in the 1940s sporting men's trousers, by the 1970s it was still generally regarded by the Establishment as shocking and unladylike.

Alongside the "Russian" collection Saint Laurent's other major collection was "China" (or "Opium") in 1977, featuring lacquer red, black, and gold on coolie hats, quilted waistcoats, and jackets with pagoda-shaped shoulders. The "Opium" perfume was released at the same time and the advertisement featuring Jerry Hall, seemingly under the influence of the eponymous narcotic, caused great offence in the US. The furore only enhanced sales even more.

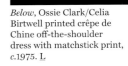

Below, Ossie Clark/Celia
Birtwell printed crêpe de
Chine off-the-shoulder
dress with matchstick print,
*c.*1975. L

OSSIE CLARK AND
CELIA BIRTWELL

Below, Ossie Clark for Radley "Traffic Light Dress", mid-1970s. F

Raymond "Ossie" Clark (1942–96) was a genius – pure and simple. He was a master technician and extremely skilled pattern cutter, with a great understanding of how to manipulate fabric. His clothes celebrate the curves of the female form, contrasting with the flat-chested gamine look of the 1960s. His wife and collaborator was the gifted textile designer Celia Birtwell (born 1941). Clark's masterly construction combined with Birtwell's prints resulted in garments of breath-taking beauty, and today they form part of every major fashion museum collection in the world.

Clark revealed and accentuated the female form, especially the breasts, and his dresses often featured self-covered buttons that fastened down the front, to be undone according to the courage of the wearer. He filled sketchbooks with delicate line drawings with titles like "Milky Way", "Guitar", "Bridget", "Acapulco", "Come Fly with Me", "Cuddly", or "Ziggy Stardust". Birtwell likewise packed sketchpads with beautiful, coloured fabric designs, also individually named.

Clark's early minidresses of 1965–66 (in heavy cotton or knitted jersey) are quite unlike the fantasia of curves and patterns that were to come. Although rare and important, buyers prefer the more fluid later examples. The Quorum boutique launched his, Birtwell's, and Alice Pollock's reputations and attracted names including John Lennon, Yoko Ono, George Harrison, Pattie Boyd (who also modelled for Clark), Mick Jagger, Bianca Jagger, and Marianne Faithfull. Some of these pieces just have the "Quorum" label, but in the late 1960s simple white satin labels were printed, bearing each of the designers' names.

Clark was a great designer but a hopeless businessman and Pollock, Quorum's owner, wasn't much better. Clark led the rock'n'roll lifestyle of his celebrity friends and in 1968 Quorum had to be rescued by Al Radley, a shrewd businessman specializing in wholesale clothing. The company now launched a mass-market, ready-to-wear line, which bore the "Ossie Clark for Radley" label, sometimes with the addition of "Print by Celia Birtwell". Whereas a Quorum dress cost £300 (approximately $480), a Radley model was priced at around £20 ($30) a garment.

Iconic cuts and prints

The most commonly found Clark/Birtwell dress, "Floating Daisies", of moss crêpe with Birtwell's "Mystic Daisy" print, sold more than 20,000. Although common, it is so striking that it always does well. Plain moss crêpe gowns with voluminous sleeves, signature curved collar, and button detailing, or smock-style with waist ties – in ivory, pale pink, blue, black, bright scarlet, or purple – are also common. These plainer gowns, though with Clark's inimitable cut, are relatively inexpensive. They usually leap in value if they use a clever colour contrast, another fabric such as satin, or at least one of Birtwell's prints.

One of Clark's most complex and valuable designs is "Ziggy Stardust", with a spiralling flounce that revolves around the body from the neck to the hem. Another highly popular and expensive model is a chiffon halter-neck dress with spaghetti-strap ties and matching cape.

Clark's more tailored Harris tweed line of forties-inspired coats and jackets, his knitwear, and suede jackets are rare, but among the least valuable of his designs. In contrast, snakeskin garments, including fitted jackets with wide lapels, diagonal zippered openings with matching miniskirts, and the few full-length maxi coats he made for friends, are highly desirable. For his close friend Nicky Samuel he combined his love of nature, astrology, and the night sky in the "Stars and Moon" dress, a tour de force of clashing colours, pink suede, snakeskin, and moss crêpe embroidered with crescent moons and stars.

After the couple's 1973 divorce, Birtwell continued to produce fabrics for Quorum until 1976 – her later designs show pointillism influences and the motifs are less flowery and more graphic, including matchstick repeats. As Clark's hedonistic lifestyle took its toll, the Radley contract was terminated and in the late 1970s he filed for bankruptcy. Despite attempts to relaunch his career, the world had moved on from romantic, flowery dresses. The one-off pieces he made while a lecturer in the late 1970s and 1980s carry a narrow black ribbon label with his name woven in gold. Usually of richly coloured draped jersey with sequined motifs, or of panne velvet cut on the bias, these late-career examples demonstrate his genius for construction and his clever use of fabrics.

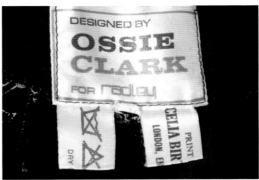

Opposite, Clark fits his "Guitar" dress from his Autumn/Winter 1971/72 collection onto his favourite model, Gala Mitchell. *Left to right,* Late 1960s and mid 1970s labels.

Below left to right, Ossie Clark snakeskin coat, late 1960s–early 1970s. L. "Floating Daisies" dress: this particular Clark/Birtwell creation sold in its tens of thousands. F. "Ziggy Stardust" dress, *c.*1977. L

ZANDRA RHODES

Opposite left to right, Early "Knitted Circle" printed chiffon kaftan robe with hood, *c*.1969. L. "Field of Lilies" printed chiffon gown, tied with a ribbon sash, *c*.1972. L. "Ayers Rock" collection evening gown, 1974. L

Below and below right, Rhodes in satin pyjamas with her signature pink hairstyle, 1978. "Zandra Rhodes" label, 1970s.

With her printed silks and chiffons showing a mastery of pattern and glorious, kaleidoscopic colour, Zandra Rhodes (born 1940) is as much an artist as a fashion designer and her timeless clothes are as wearable today as they were in the late 1960s. Adapting her hair colour, make-up, and Andrew Logan jewellery to coordinate or contrast with her latest collection, she is her own best advertisement.

Rhodes takes inspiration from a variety of sources. Her 1969 "Knitted Circle" print collection, based on knitted textiles in the Victoria & Albert Museum, was used in bright yellow felt coats with circular skirts and chiffon gowns with hoods. Although these occasionally appear on the market, they are rare – the gowns having been ripped or the felt coats devoured by moth. A 1970 New York visit led to the "Indian Feathers" collection of brightly coloured feathers on grounds, with individual feathers cut out and

reapplied as fronds on sleeve and hem edges, or made into necklaces. The 1971 "Elizabethan Silks" collection used cross-hatched patterns redolent of 16th-century slashed decorations and solid-coloured jerseys with crinkly "lettuce" edgings. "Field of Lilies", conceived in Japan and used on her dresses from 1972 onward, was her most successful print ever.

The "Shells" collection (1972–3), with its twinkling, pearlized, shell-shaped sequined details, was based on a shell-covered basket that she had discovered in a bric-a-brac store. At the same time, she reintroduced her voluminous felt coats, but now they were plain, with large sea-wave collars held in place by boning. The fabrics used in her 1973 "Ayers Rock" collection were used in dresses with quilted-satin diagonal necklines and waists. Following another American trip, for her Spring 1976 collection a cactus motif was used on chiffon and Ultrasuede chaps-like trousers and tunics. The "Mexican Turnaround" prints of 1976–7 were based on sombreros she had seen in local markets during yet another trip.

Although always focused on pattern, Rhode's aesthetic changed through the decade. 1977's "Conceptual Chic" collection (named the "punk" collection in the press) had black, red, and shocking pink jersey gowns, slashed and adorned with safety pins and bath chains, influenced by Schiaparelli and Dalí's rip-printed gown in the V&A. Her 1978 collection was again graphic – the "Painted Lady" and "Magic Heads" prints featured an almost Cubist portrait of a female face, which she used on Ultrasuede jackets and skirts to great effect.

All of Rhodes's collections from the 1970s, in particular printed chiffon gowns or pleated satin jackets, are highly desirable. Solid jersey and Ultrasuede pieces are less sought after, with the exception of those from the "punk" collection, which are quite rare. However, for dresses of the 1980s the price drops – even for fabulous chiffon examples – but they will not remain undervalued for ever and would probably make a good investment.

Opposite left to right, Grey and white printed paper taffeta ball gown, late 1960s–early 1970s: trapezoid drapes to the front skirt; the rear of the skirt with wide obi-style panels and central wine moiré ribbon. O. Ivory chiffon gown, late 1960s–early 1970s: bodice completely open at the sides, the front with demure double panel of chiffon, and with long asymmetric trained panels falling from each shoulder. N. Psychedelic chiné satin orientalist gown, c.1960: vertical slit to neck; ballooning skirt with leg holes to the sides. L

LATER MADAME GRÈS

Above left to right, Burnt-orange silk jersey sari-dress, 1979: the columnar gown with jersey overdress. L. Madame Grès in her signature turban, date unknown.

One of the greatest Parisian couturiers, Madame Grès continued her masterful construction in fabric throughout the postwar decades right up until 1988. Bucking the trend among her contemporaries, she refused lucrative licensing deals, feeling that her name was synonymous with an excellence and quality that she did not wish to see diluted. After much persuasion, she finally agreed to a ready-to-wear line in 1980, with Peggy Huyn Kinh making the models. It lasted just two seasons because Madame Grès would not compromise on her high-quality fabrics or finishes, making it impossible to produce her models economically. In 1982 she sold the profitable perfume side of her business to fund the fashion side, but the decline continued. In 1987 the company went into liquidation and in 1988 was sold to the Japanese company Yagi Tsusho, which still owns the name. Madame Grès's last collection was Spring/Summer 1988 before she retired, aged 85.

Madame Grès's gowns are timeless. She would work regardless of what else was going on in the fashion world, and repeated her designs, making only slight adjustments, for decades, so that dating her draped jersey Grecian-style gowns can be difficult. Those from the 1940s and 1950s tend to be fastened by means of hooks and eyes, while those from the 1960s onward often incorporate zip fasteners. They became increasingly revealing during the 1960s and 1970s, with the use of ties to hold the bodice in place, and could be backless, side-less, or with just two curved jersey panels to cover the breasts.

Her clothes are never boring and can often be as puzzlingly complex as a 1980s Comme des Garçons ensemble, with side slits for legs, weighted cowl necks, unusual, non-matching sleeves and draped harem-style skirts.

Her signature Grecian gowns are eminently collectable and highly sought after, though her daywear is more affordable. Contemporary designers are intrigued by her later non-draped creations with their clever cut and sometimes buy these as inspiration – Alix Grès remains a designer's designer.

A perfectionist, Jean Muir (1928–95) produced her first independent collection under the Jane & Jane label in 1962 and set up her own Jean Muir label in 1966. She is famed for her beautifully cut, draped jersey dresses with top-stitched detailing or interesting buttons and buckles. Her muse, friend, and house model the actress Joanna Lumley said of her:

> From her I learned how important it is to know the fabric and how it drapes on the female form. She was meticulous; her seamstresses worked with consummate skill, and Miss Muir, who scorned the term "designer", preferring to be called a dressmaker, would scrutinize every seam and buttonhole, her thin pale fingers pulling and turning and smoothing the finished garment. She always thought that after putting on a dress you should just forget about it and couldn't really bear the flummeries of fashion.

Muir's simple gowns come to life when put on the human form and were a hit with the working woman as they could be worn by day, and also for a smart dinner.

Although she was known for her little black dresses and draping jersey gowns, in the early part of the 1970s she also experimented with bold vibrant prints. Some of her more seductive, figure-hugging gowns can do really well at auction, but the majority are moderately priced; there is little appetite for her voluminous 1980s designs with shoulder pads. The buyers for Muir tend to be people wishing to wear them rather than museums – if they aren't sexy, they don't sell!

Left, Scarlet jersey cocktail dress, *c.*1978: plastic circlet to neck; shirred waist with peplum. F

Below left to right, Black jersey evening gown with sequined detailing, late 1970s. H. "Apples and Pears" printed chiffon dress, 1972. D

JEAN MUIR

Below, Printed crêpe de Chine dress, *c.*1970, previously owned by Joanna Lumley. I

Right, Jean Muir at New York New York nightclub, New York City, 1977.

Bianca Jagger (born 1945) was half of the golden couple of the 1970s. The Nicaraguan-born beauty was famed for her sophisticated, sharply tailored suits, which showcased a woman who knew her own mind, meant business, and was to be regarded on equal terms with her handsome rock-star spouse. She wore plunging necklines or sheer dresses with no bra – so Ossie Clark's chiffon creations were perfect for her. She was also a client and model for Zandra Rhodes, her olive skin perfectly offsetting Rhodes's pastel printed silk gowns trimmed with seashell-shaped sequins. In 1974 she was photographed wearing a beautiful Bill Gibb satin kimono dress printed with exotic birds and flowers.

However, Bianca's most famous ensemble was for her 1971 Saint-Tropez wedding to Jagger. She had firm ideas about what to wear for one of the most publicized weddings of the decade, and, instead of a traditional white, flowing bridal gown, she chose an haute couture, sharply cut, white tailored suit by Yves Saint Laurent, with no blouse underneath and a long white matching maxi skirt, accessorized with a white brimmed hat, swathed in chiffon and white silk roses, and a pair of white platform sandals. Despite showing a lot of suntanned cleavage, she

looked the quintessence of sophisticated elegance. Mick wore a traditional tailored three-piece suit... with trainers.

Another memorable garment was a red off-the-shoulder Halston dress with side slits, worn as she rode a white horse into Studio 54 in 1977, to celebrate her birthday. Roy Halston was a close friend and she often wore his one-shoulder, goddess-style draped jersey gowns – in pure white and edged with gold or jewel colours – accessorized with chunky bangles or a turban. Other favourite accessories were hats with veils and feathers, platform shoes with ankle straps (to which she would attach her Rolling Stones backstage pass), velvet chokers, and furs.

In an interview for *Harper's Bazaar* she praised her favourite designers:

Yves was my style mentor. He taught me how a jacket should fit. He played a very important role in liberating women. Suits were around before, but he showed women how to wear them. Halston had a different perspective: the American look. He wanted women to look glamorous but the line to be clean and elegant. Then came Calvin, who defined the American look; his clothes have an extraordinary simplicity and sophistication.

Style Icon

BIANCA JAGGER

"She has a great star quality." *Halston on Bianca Jagger*

What would Bianca wear? *White YSL trouser suit teamed with a striking hat *Long slinky dresses with side slits to show off her great legs *Chiffon or satin dresses with plunging necklines

When crowned British *Vogue* Designer of the Year 1970, Bill Gibb (1943–88) had recently graduated and was working for London label Baccarat. His multi-layered and multi-textured designs had an air of fantasy and romance, teaming tartans with Bakst-like black and white checks, combined with floral prints and Fair Isle knits – an implausible combination that worked!

His designs in wool crêpe, gabardine, Quiana jersey, lace, cotton for summer, stencilled leather, and knitted wool for winter, contrasted with the prevailing fashion for stiff A-line suits and dresses. Gibb injected the hippy aesthetic with the colours and textures of the Scottish Highlands and produced something new, fresh, and radical. Knit was a particular feature, specially commissioned from his friend Kaffe Fassett for ready-to-wear, or hand-knitted by Mildred Boulton for couture, and often incorporating gold or silver Lurex wools. Striking and desirable collections include the "Buddha" (Autumn/Winter 1975) and "Byzantine" (Autumn/Winter 1976) knitwear collections, and his draped jersey dresses with sequined and beaded yokes and detailing are very much in demand today.

Gibb used a bumblebee motif as his signature on enamelled buttons, belt buckles, embroidered onto dress bodices, or appliquéd onto coats and skirts. His Scottish heritage emerged in velvet doublet-style jackets and skirts embroidered with roses.

His clothes – which used the best materials and often specially commissioned prints or knits – were expensive and began to lose favour as the decade progressed. Collections dating up to around 1976 are the most desirable for collectors. His romantic, medieval-inspired gowns (the sort of dress a princess in a fairy tale might wear) with interesting prints or hand-painted birds are particularly popular, especially with museum buyers. His later collections lacked the imagination and finesse of earlier years. Although a talented designer, he was not a good businessman and, without cheaper diffusion lines, perfumes, and accessories to buoy up the core business, it eventually failed. His last collection was in 1985.

Below left and bottom, Dark blue Quiana jersey evening gown with pearlized buttons and beading, Spring/ Summer 1975. F. Enamelled bee buckles, 1970s. A

Below, Ivory wool ensemble worn by Lulu for her wedding to John Frieda in October 1976, with elaborately beaded detailing to coat shoulders and bodice. H

BILL GIBB

Clockwise from below, "Bill Gibb" label used throughout the 1970s and 1980s. Embroidered wool trouser suit, *c.*1974, with embroidered art deco shell motifs. D. "Buddha collection" ensemble with knit designed by Kaffe Fassett, Autumn/Winter 1975/76. E

Left and bottom, Vivienne Westwood in tartan bondage suit, with Jordan in a plain black version and catgirl in studded leather jacket, drainpipes, and "SEX" stilettos, 1977. A pair of red leather Seditionaries boots, *c.*1977. L. *Right*, Green and beige cotton parachute top bearing both "SEX" and "Seditionaries" labels, *c.*1976. M. Tartan bondage trousers bearing "Seditionaries Personal Collection" label, *c.*1976–7. J

VIVIENNE WESTWOOD AND MALCOLM McLAREN

Vivienne Westwood (born 1941), a school teacher with rudimentary sewing skills, and Malcolm McLaren (1946–2010), a former art student, turned fashion on its head. By using aggressive shock tactics in the clothes themselves and fusing fashion with music, they were guaranteed constant press interest, which helped spread their anarchistic mantras to teenagers the world over.

Their first shop, Let It Rock, opened at 430 King's Road in 1971. It was the antidote to "hippydom", selling fifties merchandise including records, flea market finds, vintage teddy-boy drapes and circle skirts. When the vintage clothes ran out, Westwood made her own versions in brightly coloured fabrics. As it became a destination, she stopped teaching to repair, customize and make clothes full time. The labels are narrow pink satin or white synthetic ribbon printed with the shop's name, but early labelled pieces from this era are scarce. The shop repeatedly relaunched with new identities through the 1970s.

By 1972 the duo's interest had shifted to the biker look and the shop was relaunched as Too Fast to Live Too Young to Die, in tribute to James Dean. Alongside heavily studded leather clothes, they sold motorcycle memorabilia, oil-stained second-hand Levis, custom-made zoot suits, and their first printed T-shirt "Vive Le Rock". If the clothes were labelled at all they were still "Let It Rock". Among the most coveted pieces from these early periods are Westwood's waistcoats covered in studs and chains, with slogans painted in red nail varnish, and armholes outlined with rubber from bicycle tyres and edged with fringes. Vivienne had begun to design new pieces that pleased her, rather than copying retro garments. She introduced a line of mohair sweaters and would boil up the leftover bones from the trattoria across the road, string them together to form words, and apply them to the front of black T-shirts. As only a few of these were made, they are among the most desirable of her early designs.

In 1974 the shop reopened again, this time as SEX, selling Westwood-adapted fetishistic rubber and bondage garments from specialist wholesalers alongside Westwood's own range of clothing. From 1972–9 they evolved their famous T-shirts emblazoned

with inflammatory slogans, which delivered anti-fashion messages and served as a clarion call to rebellion. Buying white T-shirts in bulk, Westwood painstakingly deconstructed them, cutting off arms, slitting open shoulders, and slashing the necks. Alternatively, she would cut two large squares of cotton jersey that she sewed up at the sides and shoulders. The first SEX Original T-shirts were printed by hand on Westwood's kitchen table using a children's printing set and stencils. Malcolm devised the images and text, pilfering scandalous material from political, social, and sexual sources. Vivienne customized them with see-through plastic pockets and zips to reveal nipples. In the autumn of 1974 they introduced one bearing a manifesto "You're gonna wake up one morning and know what side of the bed you've been lying on!" with lists of their loves and hates below. By now the clothes bore a large pink label woven with "SEX Original" in blue lettering.

Their controversial 1975 "Cambridge Rapist" T-shirt attracted a wave of negative publicity. Of course this fuelled demand and large numbers were made over the following years so that today they are one of the more commonly found designs. Styled by McLaren, Westwood, and Jordan (the shop's manager), the Sex Pistols were formed that year and their radical look served as a brilliant marketing tool. "So long as the band has the right look," McLaren observed, "the music doesn't matter too much."

By 1976 the T-shirts (now including Dick Turpin, Disney characters committing obscene acts, semi-naked cowboys, and "Tits") and muslin bondage shirts were being screen-printed to keep up with demand. A staff member, Alan Jones, was arrested for gross indecency for wearing the Cowboys T-shirt in Piccadilly Circus and the shop was raided. Regardless, the shirts continued to be sold but were hidden under the counter. They remade cotton army trousers in black satin with a towelling "bum flap" and bondage straps, and went on to make versions in red, white, and blue cotton, and tartan wool. Westwood had discovered her metier as a designer and her creativity flourished.

In 1976 punk rock had become a major player in the music scene with groups including the Buzzcocks and the Clash, as well as the Sex Pistols, entering the charts. The shop was relaunched as Seditionaries, "for heroes, prostitutes and dykes". Westwood wanted to, "seduce people to revolt". The label changed to a narrow black silk ribbon, often applied to T-shirt shoulders or to the breast pockets of bondage suits. The broad white satin "Personal Collection" labels appeared inside the heavier parachute or bondage tops or were sandwiched below layers of muslin on bondage shirts with elongated straitjacket-style sleeves with clip fastenings. The range had expanded to include cotton shirts with Peter Pan or vinyl collars, woollen schoolboy blazers with all the seams on display, towelling jackets, hangman sweaters of knitted string, donkey trousers of needle-cord with Westwood's trademark zippered crotches that went from the front to the back, red denim drainpipe jeans with plastic see-through pockets, black leather boots with spikes and studs, strappy black patent stilettos, and handkerchiefs printed with images of the

Queen with swastika eyes or safety-pinned nose. Good quality and well made, the clothes were expensive, resulting in a high incidence of shoplifting (which Westwood didn't seem to mind) and numerous DIY copies.

Perhaps Westwood's most tasteless stunt was to release the "She's Dead. I'm Alive. I'm Yours" T-shirt and Sid Vicious "Action Man", complete with coffin, following the Sex Pistols' disastrous 1978 tour (when Vicious killed his girlfriend Nancy Spungen). By the end of the decade punk had run its course and in 1979 Seditionaries closed its doors on its punk aficionados. In the mid 1980s Westwood leased her punk designs to a nearby shop called BOY (formerly ACME Attractions). They ignored stipulations on labelling and so large numbers of seemingly genuine Seditionaries T-shirts flooded the market, especially in Japan where Westwood/McLaren creations were (and are) highly coveted. As prices at auction escalated around 2005, modern fake Westwood/McLaren T-shirts and clothing became a real problem.

Below left, A Westwood/McLaren "Cambridge Rapist" T-shirt, *c.*1975–6: "Seditionaries" ribbon label to left sleeve, inside-out, with green mask portrait, musical notes, picture and death announcement of Brian Epstein in shades of pink and green. E

Below, "God Save the Queen" printed muslin T-shirt, Seditionaries, *c.*1977: inset with "Personal Collection" label at the front hip. G

Right, A rare Westwood/
McLaren Let it Rock black
leather waistcoat, *c.*1971:
un-labelled, with bicycle tyre
edges to the armholes, white
nylon fringes, the reverse
with "Rebel" written in red
nail varnish, Harley Davidson
silk badge appliquéd above,
"Elvis" written in studs to the
hem. P

The 1980s was a curious decade that simultaneously gave rise to a host of different looks – from the status-symbol power suit to the ethereal deconstructed creations of avant-garde Japanese designers, and from the dressing-up box of the New Romantics with its frills, pirate hats, and highwayman's frock coats to the futuristic minimalist outfits worn by the German group Kraftwerk. It seems we had it all.

It is with the power suit, however, that the decade is most commonly associated. These tailored suits for men and women had large jackets, padded shoulders, and sleeves that were intentionally designed to be rolled back (even on expensive Armani suits). Men's trousers were high-waisted and often peg-topped Kid Creole style. Jeans were also high-waisted and cut high at the ankle, often to reveal white socks. Skirts were generally tight and could be super-mini or knee-length.

The big-shouldered, super-glamorous styles worn by the characters of the US soap *Dynasty* popularized power dressing globally. Colours were bold and brash and often contrasted with black. Prestigious designer logos were proudly displayed on the outside of shirts and jackets, illustrating vulgar status-symbol dressing at its worst. It was the decade that really launched the "designer label" and major American and European fashion houses mass produced expensive ready-to-wear on a global scale.

Sports influenced everyday casual wear with colourful shell suits, designer trainers, and leggings worn with stilettos. Jane Fonda's aerobics and the 1980 film *Fame* made leotards, "bodies", and leggings part of the ordinary wardrobe. Oversized slogan T-shirts were all the rage: Katherine Hamnett famously wore her "58% DON'T WANT PERSHING" anti-nuclear T-shirt when she met Mrs Thatcher at Downing Street in 1984.

The Sloane Ranger look, epitomized by Lady Diana Spencer, included frilled, pie-crust-collar blouses, a string of pearls, Laura Ashley skirts, pashmina shawls, polo shirts, Barbour jackets (collar up), and Ferragamo pumps with bows or gold hardware.

Eveningwear featured brightly coloured printed-silk cocktail gowns with ruched gathers, large bows, and puffball skirts (introduced by Lacroix in 1986 in the wake of Westwood's mini-crini). Chanel's Karl Lagerfeld made a feature of the Chanel chain belt, and gold became the key accent. Yves Saint Laurent used brilliantly coloured appliqués in his "Picasso" collections (Autumn/Winter 1979/80 and Spring/Summer 1988) and layered shocking pink tutu-like petticoats under short velvet cocktail dresses.

Hair was large and permed for both men and women. Inspired by the likes of Nick Rhodes and Adam Ant, dramatic, full make-up was also worn by the more fashionable young men, with heavily accentuated kohl-rimmed eyes. Accessories played a major role with massive droplet or stud earrings, logo-emblazoned designer sunglasses, gold-linked multi-chained belts, and wide leather cummerbunds. Hats – which had fallen from favour since the 1950s – became important again as part of the overall look, as did matching gloves and shoes.

Avant-garde fashion

In contrast, a new generation of independently minded Japanese designers – Rei Kawakubo, Yohji Yamamoto, and Issey Miyake – debuted in Paris in 1981 to mixed reactions. Challenging the accepted Western concept of beauty,

Below, Yves Saint Laurent Rive Gauche leopard-print satin cocktail suit, Autumn/Winter 1986/87. F

THE ECLECTIC EIGHTIES

"I put long over short, short over long, and break every possible rule and find different looks emerge by playing with how they are put on the body... fashion has never been so exciting." *John Galliano*

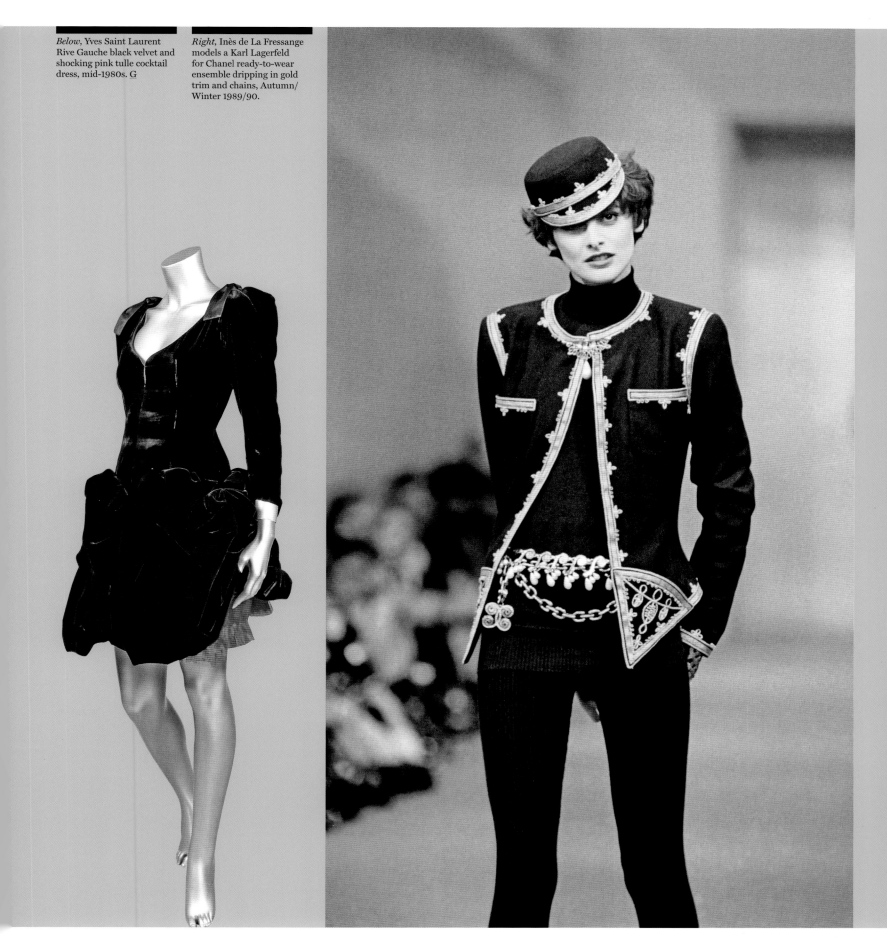

Below, Yves Saint Laurent Rive Gauche black velvet and shocking pink tulle cocktail dress, mid-1980s. G

Right, Inès de La Fressange models a Karl Lagerfeld for Chanel ready-to-wear ensemble dripping in gold trim and chains, Autumn/ Winter 1989/90.

Below, Christian Lacroix rose-print cocktail dress, late 1980s–early 1990s: gold label; the full skirt adorned with black-and-white ruffles and rosettes, complete with stiffened crinoli

Below right, Slogan T-shirts were a feature of the mid-1980s as pioneered by Katherine Hamnett. This "Feed the World" T-shirt was made to coincide with the Aid concert in 1985. B

they preached "deconstruction" whereby the very structure and finish of a garment was questioned and altered. Clothes in a monotone palette were adorned with holes, rips, slashes, frays, and tears, *Le Figaro* reported that the Japanese designers produced clothes "for the end of the world that look as if they have been bombed to shreds".

Also in contrast to the power-suited *Dynasty*-style fashions were the multi-layered, avant-garde looks advocated by the likes of BodyMap, John Galliano, and Vivienne Westwood. Many of these more outrageous looks were both influenced and adopted by the "New Romantic" movement (as it has come to be known), which had its roots in the 1980s club scene.

Far left, Richard Torry padded black satin armour-style jacket, early 1980s: the shoulder treatment is similar to that used in Westwood's 1988 "Time Machine" collection. E

Centre, Rare Christopher Nemeth/Judy Blame evening coat, *c.*1985. This came with a matching Judy Blame single earring with tassels, safety pins and buttons. N

THE NEW ROMANTICS

Above, Rare Leigh Bowery star coat, "Pakis in Outer Space" collection, 1982: the back inset with large central star, the front panels cut away in late 18th-century-style and fastened by three buttons. L

In its more mainstream form, the New Romantic look was exemplified by the pretty, crinoline-style ball gowns made by Elizabeth and David Emanuel and Zandra Rhodes – all bows and ruffles and dressing-up box girliness. At its most cutting edge were clothes designed by Richard Torry, Stevie Stewart, Christopher Nemeth, David Holah, Rachel Auburn, Leigh Bowery, Melissa Caplan's Pallium Products label, and Rosemary Turner's "Toy Soldier" styles (from PX in London's Covent Garden). These were worn by the likes of Toyah Wilcox, Stephen Linard, Stephen Jones, and Judy Blame. At PX, Steve Strange was shop assistant and Stephen Jones sold fantastical hats in the basement. Sue Clowes sold her brilliantly coloured prints incorporating Jewish and Christian iconography through The Foundry where Boy George was shop assistant.

It was a subculture that dominated fashion and pop music. Venues such as the Cha Cha club run by Scarlett Bordello, the Taboo Club fronted by the outrageous performance artist and fashion designer Leigh Bowery, and the famous Blitz club fronted by the 19-year-old Steve Strange, granted admission only if you were dressed in an avant-garde, highly individual, or creative manner. If you were square, you couldn't get in. The aficionados were called the "Blitz Kids", and the ideas, the experimentation, and theatricality of the clothes they wore passed from club to catwalk and were disseminated worldwide.

Today fashion pieces by Leigh Bowery (1961–94), the most extreme and talented of the group, are particularly highly prized. Some of the other Blitz Kid designers, though highly collectable, are still moderately priced but this is an important niche collecting area and is probably worth investing in for the future. These small independent designers did not have massive outputs and were active for a relatively short time – and are consequently rare.

Above, Boy George wearing a Susan Clowes T-shirt with Hebrew script and roses.

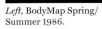
Below, White stretch-velvet and black rib-knit dress, c.1985. I

BODYMAP

Below, Printed turquoise cotton jersey dress and label, *c.*1985, with low, plunging back and elongated sleeves. E

Stevie Stewart and David Holah (both born 1958) launched BodyMap in 1982. Stewart said: "In the beginning of the eighties it was very grey out there, we came along full of fresh and vibrant ideas with new proportions and interesting prints and fabrics and it was all well received!"

The look was casual and multi-layered, but also dramatic with an experimental approach to scale. Made of specially developed cotton/lycra/viscose jersey, the construction was ground-breaking. Stewart said: "We turned pattern cutting on its head and tried to develop our own techniques – for example upside down sleeves and throwback neck holes, one-seam skirts, petal fishtail skirts, and oversized sweatshirt tops. We often took the concepts of the collections right through to pattern cutting shapes – for example the 'Cat in the Hat Takes a Rumble with the Techno Fish' (Autumn/Winter 1984/85) had fish-like pattern shapes."

Voluminous coats were printed with "BodyMap" in giant lettering and teamed with a skin-tight mermaid-shaped skirt, with a rah-rah skirt, or a baby-doll-shaped "Barbee" top with ruffled hem and stockings. The composition of the overall look was not prescribed but up to the individual. You could add hats, bras, tights, leggings, and Converse-style trainers with wedge heels.

In the early years textile designer Hilde Smith created computer-aided designs for BodyMap's distinctively bold graphic prints, which included stars, cross-hatched patterns, and strong square repeats with infills. The collection names were as ingenious as the clothes and included "Barbee Takes a Trip Around Nature's Cosmic Curves" (Spring/Summer 1985; featuring acid colours and synthetics) and "Querelle Meets Olive Oil" (Spring/Summer 1984; combining the gawkiness of Olive Oil with the sexuality of Querelle). Boy George, Leigh Bowery, and dancer Michael Clark modelled the clothes on the catwalk. In 1985 BodyMap launched the B Basic junior line and Red Label (a less expensive line) as well as swimwear. Their ranges were aimed not just at clubbers, but internationally at avant-garde boutique clientele. The company closed in the late 1980s, their niche market having struggled to survive in recessionary times.

Finding good condition examples can be difficult because they are often faded from multiple washes. The pieces bearing the white and black woven label with a handprint are the most coveted, while garments combining the strong prints with an interesting cut are highly prized by museums and collectors alike.

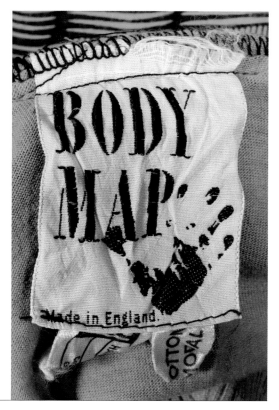

THIERRY MUGLER

Left, Pleated cloth-of-gold cocktail gown, *c.*1987: with fan pleats radiating from the centre waist, front and back; exaggerated angular shoulders; and horizontally pleated sleeves. <u>P</u>

Below and bottom, Metallic evening ensemble, *c.*1987–9: the strapless boned bodice with curls and fins; the matching trained fishtail skirt with gill-like panels. <u>S</u>. Purple suede and black patent jacket, Spring/Summer 1989. <u>N</u>

Thierry Mugler's distinctive power dressing with a fetishist edge produced sexy and figure-hugging styles for the empowered modern woman, accentuating the curves of the female torso, whether in a simple office suit by day or a metallic mermaid evening gown by night.

Thierry Mugler (born 1948) launched his first personal collection, "Café de Paris", in Paris in 1973 and opened his first boutique in the place des Victoires in 1978. The 1970s garments bear brown satin labels, while those made after around 1980 are blue. The early seventies pieces are rare, but it was in the 1980s that Mugler really flourished. With spectacular, theatrical catwalk shows and celebrity clients both on and off the stage, he became a superstar.

Exaggerated shoulders, nipped-in waists, peplums, hip-hugging pencil skirts, and corsets are trademark looks. The widened shoulders combined with narrow pencil skirts formed a triangular silhouette that would soften during the 1990s with curved shoulders and an hourglass figure. Mugler injected Dior's New Look with a futuristic, sci-fi glamour. Jerry Hall epitomized his aesthetic ideal, and Mugler said of her: "She has it all, sensuality, gentleness, voluptuousness and disdain."

Mugler's clothes have an air of fantasy and fetish. His daywear in the form of chic, sexy business suits was commercially successful and made in large numbers. These can be relatively inexpensive today. He liked to use black and would mix textures, so black gabardine or jersey could be teamed with black velvet and, later, vinyl. The more brightly coloured examples tend to be slightly pricier. Fins running down the sides of sleeves and wing shapes are another typical touch. He loved stars and these appear as cutwork or differently coloured inserts in the clothes – as elaborate rhinestone-studded comets on velvet dresses and suits; as studs on the communist-style dresses of his "Les Milteuses" collection (Autumn/Winter 1986/87); and as stylized buckles and jewellery – from simple metal brooches and earrings right up to the elaborate enamelled-metal "Milky Way" articulated necklace made by the Parisian haute couture jeweller Robert Goossens.

However, it is in eveningwear that Mugler allows his fantasy and imagination free rein. His clothes are alternately reminiscent of those worn by a Cleopatra-like empress (with finely pleated skirts radiating from girdle-like hip panels), a subterranean mermaid (with metallic scale-like tiers to the skirt and curling shell-like breasts), or a comic-book hero (see 1989's brilliantly coloured suede jackets inset with cobwebs of lustrous black patent leather).

Mugler's success continued into the 1990s but in 2000 he closed his atelier. A new generation rediscovered his mastery in the Metropolitan Museum of Art's 2008 "Superheroes: Fashion and Fantasy" exhibition and his artistic direction of Beyoncé's 2009 "I Am …" world tour.

"Every woman has a goddess inside her. I love to glorify her."
Thierry Mugler

Having trained in Paris with the great Jean Dessès and Guy Laroche, Valentino Garavani (born 1932) opened his fashion house in the prestigious via Condotti in Rome in 1959. The influential San Francisco department store I. Magnin established him as a household name in the United States, and when Jacqueline Kennedy married Aristotle Onassis in his ivory crêpe and lace-banded minidress, 38 couture versions were reportedly ordered.

He enhanced his worldwide brand prominence with Valentino boutiques (launched 1969), ready-to-wear lines Miss V and Valentino Night, and franchises in leather goods, jewellery, and perfume. There is a plentiful supply of well-made ready-to-wear at moderate prices, but values leap for his superb haute couture (alta moda) creations.

In the late 1970s and early 1980s his elegant, beautifully crafted, obviously expensive gowns with fabulous embroidery or exquisite beading were prized by rich clients. Valentino always used the best possible fabrics often in combinations of rich colours, though his name will always be synonymous with red. If you have to own just one Valentino dress, then try to make it a red haute couture one!

His fellow Italian, Roberto Capucci (born 1930), a genius at colour combinations and contrasts, also achieved great success in America. He opened his Rome fashion house in 1950, moving to rue Cambon, Paris in 1962 where he remained until returning to Italy in 1969 to escape what he considered to be the overly fickle, critical Paris press. From the 1960s onward he experimented with materials, mixing plastic and glass, or bamboo canes and silk jersey, with great panache, style, and perfection of line. He has made gowns with stiffened three-dimensional petals forming the skirt, and entirely of crimped and goffered silk taffeta. Some of his more elaborate evening gowns can be viewed as stand-alone sculptures, with no need of a body at all! Couture Capucci is rare but these masterly creations are highly desirable, appealing as attention-grabbing red carpet gowns and to museums requiring a spectacularly colourful, show-stopping piece.

Below left, Roberto Capucci couture black velvet cocktail dress, mid-1980s, with flounced flamenco hem lined in brilliant colours. The skirt of this dress descends in multicoloured wave-like forms – Capucci used strong colours to emphasize or exaggerate the construction elements of his clothes. L

Below right, Valentino couture black velvet cocktail dress with angular shoulders, early 1980s, couture labelled: a deep band of rhinestone and jet-beaded strapwork encases the lower back, forming points at the front to accentuate the narrow waist. N

ITALIAN MASTERS

Right, Valentino couture jade green satin and sequined cocktail dress, *c.*1983: the zip-fronted bodice embroidered and sequined with interlocking leaf forms in shades of blue, green, and silver, edged in black chenille. Valentino's couture clothes are of exquisite quality and finish, comparable with anything produced in the best Paris fashion houses. **M**

Diana, Princess of Wales (1961–97) was one of the most iconic, photographed fashion figures of the 20th century. Wherever she went, her style was minutely scrutinized, discussed, and imitated. As a young "Sloane Ranger", Lady Diana Spencer wore demure blouses with pie-crust frilled collars and simple gathered skirts. However, in March 1981, on her first official engagement with Prince Charles, there were intimations that inside this shy young woman was an embryonic style icon just waiting to emerge. She wore a black taffeta Emanuel gown with strapless bodice and plunging neckline, her daring décolleté revealed to the awaiting press against a glare of frenzied camera flash bulbs. The Emanuels also made the most important dress of all – the ivory silk taffeta creation she wore for her marriage to Prince Charles at Saint Paul's Cathedral on 29 July 1981.

In the early years of her marriage the Princess favoured romantic ball gowns or pretty, delicately printed chiffon cocktail dresses. Her taste in clothes matured with her, however, and she took to wearing rich, dark velvets, which acted as the perfect foil for her fine jewels and English-rose complexion. She often wore black, despite advice that it was against royal protocol.

By the 1990s the Princess's self-confidence had grown. She wore more sculpted, figure-skimming clothes that emphasized and enhanced her slim, athletic physique, and her outfits became more daring and sophisticated. Although still loyal to her favourite British designers – Catherine Walker, Zandra Rhodes, Victor Edelstein, Bellville Sassoon, Bruce Oldfield, and Jacques Azagury – she began to wear clothes by foreign designers such as Gianni Versace and Christina Stambolian.

Below, The black Emanuel taffeta evening gown worn by Lady Diana Spencer for her first official appearance (after the engagement announcement) in the company of HRH Prince Charles at Goldsmiths' Hall, 9 March 1981. FF

Right and far right, Catherine Walker pink sequined ivory crêpe gown with asymmetric neckline worn by the Princess in 1991. The figure-hugging dress showed to great effect the toned physique of the Princess, whose choice of dress would become ever more confident and sensuous during the 1990s. This dress combines glamour with elegant sophistication. AA. The Princess wearing a Catherine Walker silk crêpe evening gown, July 1989.

Style Icon

DIANA, PRINCESS OF WALES

"It's vital that the monarchy keeps in touch with the people. It's what I try and do." *Diana, Princess of Wales*

AZZEDINE ALAÏA

Above, Alaïa celebrating the
female form – models in
Paris, October 1986.

Although Azzedine Alaïa (born 1939) had been designing in Paris since the 1970s, he first came to prominence after launching his "Alaïa" label in 1980. While other designers were experimenting with layers and volume, he was one of the first exponents of body-conscious dressing. His clothes hugged the wearer, emphasized curves, and complemented slim, athletic figures. Early collections were mainly black, sometimes with solid-coloured ivory, grey, brown, turquoise, almond green, or purple. Although ready-to-wear, his clothes were expensive and initially produced to ensure that demand outstripped supply. Although he introduced a few patterned knits in the early 1990s, he prefers his clothes to be about construction and texture rather than pattern. His skimpy, skin-tight knitted black jersey dresses with highly structured seamed panels have become a design classic.

Alaïa is a genius with knit and in the 1980s used it in various forms – straightforward fine wool jersey, soft tufted and ribbed chenille, or slithering silk. One of his most iconic pieces is a 1985 knitted gown with hood, made famous by Grace Jones. Another knitted dress completely spirals around the body and unzips to form a strip of flat fabric. This was inspired by the French actress Arletty in the 1938 film *Hôtel du Nord* – "she wore a zipper dress," Alaïa has said, "and when she unzipped it, she made a gesture that intrigued me. It is from this gesture that I developed the idea of this dress which is completely flat when open."

Another favourite material is leather, which Alaïa has used since the late 1970s. It can be plain but luxuriously soft with clever gored, top-stitched panelling; punched with holes and riveted; piped in a contrasting colour; or laser-cut to look like lace. He uses it on coats and skirts, and for entire dresses, sometimes with wide fold-over lapels and massive zips. In Autumn/Winter 1981/82 Alaïa introduced the widely copied "body". They can be of plain knitted viscose; elaborate cocktail dresses of leopard weave tulle and velvet; or complex affairs featuring multiple straps or fastenings.

Although separates and plain day suits remain reasonably accessible, his ground-breaking, eighties eveningwear is understandably desirable and highly sought after. Alaïa is a great fashion historian and collector (his fitted day suits might, for example, take their inspiration from a 19th-century riding habit or corset). His expertise in historical dress is renowned and his private collection of vintage fashion and haute couture is one of the best in the world, each piece selected for its beauty, rarity, and excellence of design. His heroes are Madeleine Vionnet and Cristóbal Balenciaga, whose craftsmanship he matches in his own work.

Right, Rare hooded dress of chocolate brown knitted wool, *c.*1986: with single zip that circles the body. Grace Jones, the model and performer, was famous for wearing Alaïa's signature hooded knit gowns. K

JOHN GALLIANO

"There are few truly creative people in the fashion world who, through their spirit, their creative joy and their personalities, really give fashion what it needs – some inventive madness." *Anna Wintour on Galliano*

John Galliano (born 1960) takes endless inspiration from historical fashion and voraciously experiments with cut and construction. The clever and unusual shapes of his 1980s pieces are immediately apparent and scale plays a big part, with shirts wide enough for two, sleeves cut in curves and inset with ruffles, and major design features on details such as pockets and buttons.

His graduation collection (1984) celebrated the extravagant, anarchistic, and revealing clothing of *les incroyables* and *les merveilleuses* – the royalist subculture of fashionable young men and women in post-revolutionary, late 18th-century Paris. Through nocturnal "researches" into London's club scene, Galliano was part of the movement away from aggressive, hardline punk toward frills, decadence, and romance. Ivory, beige, and grey clothes were injected with coloured stripes, scarlet linings, floral, sprigged dandyish waistcoats, and tricolour rosettes, to form a loose, fluid, layered romantic look. Billowing white organdie shirts with cravat bows were worn under contrasting waistcoats and draped asymmetric outsized coats. Jersey trousers were cut baggy and draped, with low-slung crotches, the fabric fitting closer as it descended the leg. Browns, London bought the entire collection and the more wearable

waistcoats and organdie shirts were a sell out, enabling Galliano to begin manufacturing the clothes at home with the help of friends. These rare early pieces just have cheap printed ribbon labels bearing his name.

Galliano's second collection, "Afghanistan Repudiates Western Ideals" (Spring/Summer 1985), featured cotton dhoti-style trousers in pale beige, denim blue, grey, brown checks, and coloured stripes. These were worn with voluminous tailcoats with leg o' mutton sleeves that extended to act "like gloves". Other sleeves were cut in a C-curve and slashed from wrist to cuff, caught with buttons, and edged in puckered, ruched bands of the same fabric.

"A mad mix"
Mismatched lapels featured on coats and cropped bolero jackets. One coat was worn upside down and made to look inside out with visible bias-bound seams, and numerous jackets had DA (duck's arse) hems, while some featured handmade blue and green hardened Plasticine buttons. Alongside were ultra-long jersey dresses, tubular skirts, and long-johns-style knitted cotton breeches. Galliano commented: "It's all a mad mix. Everything is off balance ... I mix shapes, mix proportions." For this, his first major commercial collection, burgundy labels were woven with "John

Galliano 1" and a coat of arms in blue. The collection was not mass-produced, and Galliano simply took wholesale material to clothing workshops to make the garments quickly and cheaply.

"The Ludic Games" (Autumn/Winter 1985/86) was mainly in shades of white and ivory and marked the beginning of his long-term collaboration with creative consultant Amanda Harlech, who helped to make his shows unmissable theatrical "happenings". Intended to be worn inside out and upside down, some of the unisex dresses could also be worn back to front and included bias-cut empire styles with curved sleeves and headgear that included floral wreaths, twigs, and stuffed birds.

Models in Spring/Summer 1986's "Fallen Angels" (the start of a seven-collection collaboration with accessories designer Patrick Cox) had whitened faces stamped with Galliano's logo and wore dampened white muslin empire-line dresses. "Forgotten Innocents" (Autumn/Winter 1986/87) showcased "alternative ways of putting clothes together... [Galliano] was experimenting with circular cutting, which causes wonderful stress to fabric, and attenuated drapes but without tucking." Financial backing (from Aguecheek) for Spring/Summer 1987 led to a more refined

Below, Tartan waistcoat, probably made for Browns, London, after the success of his 1984 graduate collection. Here Galliano uses a simple, cheap satin label (right), as this is before his first properly launched and financed collections. The back is cut very high and formed from two kinds of floral cotton. I

style in which billowing shirts were scaled down and the stylized rose, the DA, twisted fabrics, and a pastel or subdued palette of colours all became recognizable trademarks.

Pieces from Galliano's early collections are difficult to find, because of the perceived complexity of his cut, there was no mass-production. Dogged by financial problems after 1990 he continued to produce collections that he couldn't always afford to show – until Anna Wintour paved the way for his 1993 show (made entirely in black cloth, the only fabric he *could* afford). After a brief stint as head designer at Givenchy (from Spring 1996), he joined Dior as head of design with a triumphant first collection in Spring 1997, a success he continued until his high-profile dismissal in 2011.

A controversial figure, Galliano remains one of the greatest designers of the 20th century, his work highly regarded by fashion museums and collectors the world over. Because his early collections were not mass-produced, they are rare and already sell for high sums at auction, as do his couture designs from his early career at Dior.

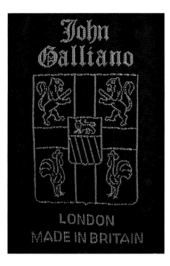

Left and bottom left, "John Galliano London" woven label before his move to Paris in 1993. Galliano's very early labels also followed this design with the addition of a "1" after the designer's name. Fine John Galliano mustard cotton jacket, mid-1980s: with padded angular shoulders, long gothic sleeves, and large oval button at the fitted waist; piped in dark green. L

Below left to right, Charcoal-grey cotton smock dress, 1985/86, labelled "John Galliano 1": the midriff with four drawstring ties, some edged with fur pompoms that cause the front of the skirt to ruffle and rise. L. Beige cotton voluminous coat, 1987: wide, high lapels; double-breasted with mother-of-pearl buttons; pockets inset high and wide to the chest. L

Right, Models dressed in white from Galliano's "Forgotten Innocents" collection, Autumn/Winter 1986/87.

WESTWOOD IN
THE EIGHTIES

In 1980 Westwood and McLaren relaunched their shop at 430 Kings Road as World's End, a combination of Dickensian curiosity shop and lurching galleon, complete with tilted floor. The new label read "Westwood McLaren. Born in England" and showed an out-thrust pirate's arm wielding a curved cutlass.

Moving away from all things Punk and towards Romanticism, Westwood came into her own as a designer. In the "Pirate" collection (Autumn/Winter 1981/82) she reinterpreted and experimented with historical dress, ethnic cuts and patterns. Dominated by the unisex pirate shirt and the famous "squiggle" print (adapted from an original Jean-Charles de Castelbajac design), it featured low-slung, roomy half-mast trousers, damask and madras-striped jackets, and black bicorne felt hats trimmed with gold tassels and cockades. Some of the more rare and expensive footwear was made in rich brocades, worn with printed cotton stockings. Monochrome satin doublet-shaped waistcoats balanced the riot of colours and layers. Their first London catwalk show was featured in British *Vogue* – the *enfants terrible* of British fashion had gone mainstream. Although individual Pirate components are relatively inexpensive, entire ensembles (expensive even at the time) are rare and museums desperate to acquire complete versions can push bidding to five figures.

The "Savages" collection (Spring/Summer 1982) mixed ethnic and Dickensian themes. Long white cotton jersey togas, with trained skirts knotted on one side, were printed with well-known paintings. These are especially desirable for their fusion of fashion and art. Accessories included round felt hats and burqa-style veils. Boldly coloured geometric knits, printed cotton dresses, skirts, and tunics made a riot of colour.

"Nostalgia of Mud" (or "Buffalo") (Autumn/Winter 1982/83) saw Rastafarian and primitivist clothes cut deliberately large so that models had to hold them in place. Satin bras were worn atop printed cotton toga-dresses as well as thick, layered skirts printed with figures, shoes like leather bags tied around the ankles, and tall, felt Bolivian-style "mountain hats", the whole collection in muted browns, pinks, and greys.

"Punkature" (Spring/Summer 1983) was described in the press as "bag-lady chic" – a fusion of punk and buffalo styles which included complicated prints, distressed fabrics in arsenic green, oranges, browns, shocking pinks, and blues, and simple, voluminous shapes. Playing with proportion and scale, shirts had yokes of contrasting fabric, impossibly wide necks, and extra-long sleeves. Skirts and trousers had hobo-style bib fronts with buttoned straps, some made from dishcloth fabric. Brightly coloured open-toed socks were worn with sandals. Printed skirts and shirts featured scenes from the movie *Blade Runner* (1982). Not hugely successful, the collection is consequently quite rare.

The "Witches" collection, Autumn/Winter 1983/84 was Westwood and McLaren's last collaboration. Ground-breaking and dynamic, it was characterized by masculine tailoring, striped wool suitings, peaked and pointed shoulders, rubber phallus-shaped buttons, and comfortable sweatpants stencilled with Buffalo-girl motifs. Keith Haring designs adorned jackets, skirts, and fluorescent jacquard knitwear. Pointed felt chico-hats (after Chico Marx) and leather trainers with double or triple tongues by Patrick Cox completed the look. It was extreme, but wearable, and commercially successful.

For "Hypnos" (Spring/Summer 1984) production moved to Italy and was financed

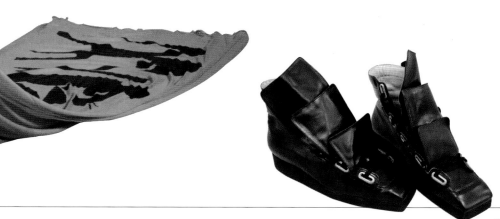

by the Italian entrepreneur Carl D'Amario. It used fluorescent stretch synthetics with white or black contrasts, again using rubber phallus buttons and prints of Medusa heads with phalluses in place of snakes. Commercially, the collection flopped and World's End, and the second shop Nostalgia of Mud, were forced to close. The following season's "Clint Eastwood" collection featured fluorescent belted macs and short-legged bondage trousers smothered in Italian logos and Day-Glo patches. Little was actually made of this collection after its chaotic Paris showing. Nonetheless, D'Amario continued to financially support the World's End label.

The "Mini-Crini" collection (Spring/Summer 1985) featured tweed and cotton skirts in meticulously researched Victorian style. Unlike the prevailing focus on the shoulders, Westwood emphasised the hips. In black and white or printed with stars and stripes, the skirts were worn with spotted shirts, white Minnie Mouse shoes or black leather rocking horse shoes. Because only small numbers were made, complete mini-crini ensembles rarely come onto the market.

In 1986 Vivienne returned to London and World's End. Her "Harris Tweed" collection (Autumn/Winter 1987/88) used specially commissioned tweeds made in the Scottish Hebrides. Beautifully tailored jackets and knitted twinsets, accessorized with Harris tweed crowns, rocking horse shoes, pearly queen hats for women and deerstalkers for men, gently parodied refined Establishment styles. She devised a new label with a Saturn-like ring added to the Harris Tweed orb trademark which she had adopted. The motif was also embroidered onto the knitted twinsets by John Smedley. From now on her clothing bore red labels for standard ready-to-wear and gold for the more expensive special orders, couture, and Italian-made main line.

The Pagan Series (Spring 1988–Spring 1990) consisted of "Britain Must Go Pagan", "Time Machine", "Civilizade", "Voyage to Cythera", and "Pagan V", but only "Time Machine" – featuring Fair Isle Space Invader-patterned sweaters and waistcoats and jackets with removable articulated panelled sleeves, all in tweeds, striped wool, black leather, and sheepskin for both men and women – was commercially successful. Metallic corsets with detachable armour sleeves and miniskirts with detachable tulle ruffles that caused the front pleats to stick out also featured. One of her most famous pieces is the headline-grabbing nude body stocking with mirrored fig leaf from the "Voyage to Cythera" collection (Autumn/Winter 1989/90) in which Westwood was memorably photographed.

All of Westwood's 1980s output is extremely collectable. Her imagination, historic narrative, clever construction, use of traditional fabrics in new ways (and new fabrics in traditional ways), and the high quality of her garments (even during the punk years), ensures her place as one of the greatest and most influential designers of the 20th century.

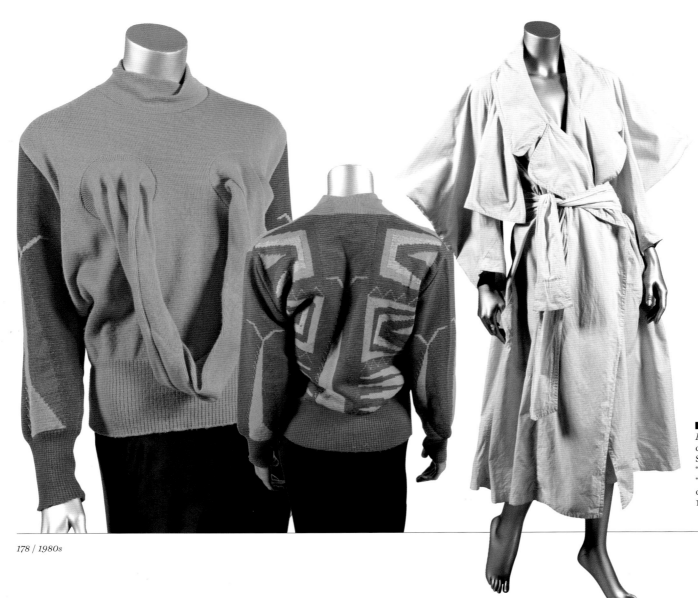

Left to right, "Savages" collection boob-tube sweater, Spring/Summer 1982, with "World's End" label. E. "Witches" collection trench coat, Autumn/Winter 1983/84. L

Right, "Pirate" ensemble from Autumn/Winter 1981/82: shown here are the fabulous bicorne hat, squiggle-print shirt and waistcoat, but this rare complete ensemble also includes red damask jacket and trousers and chisel-toed pirate boots. U

Although Kenzo Takada, Issey Miyake, and Hanae Mori were already well-established fashion names in Paris by the 1980s, they designed and made what were essentially European clothes, seen through Japanese eyes. However, in the early 1980s the "big three" – Rei Kawakubo (born 1942; founder of Comme des Garçons), Yohji Yamamoto (born 1943), and Issey Miyake (born 1938) – introduced a whole new, purely Japanese, way of looking at fashion, their considered, intellectual approach far removed from anything in the West.

Kawakubo and Yamamoto came to international prominence in 1981 when they showed their first collections in Paris. Almost entirely black, both collections featured oversized, asymmetric, distressed garments. Black, which lends itself to accentuating the silhouette, was the favourite colour, sometimes punctuated with ivory or grey. The fabrics themselves, the way they fell, the shadows they created, the interplay with the

human figure, were all taken into account when a garment was designed. Some of the clothes were so complicated that the various ways of wearing them were not always clear, but in the main their principal beauty lay in their simplicity, texture, layers, and volume.

The ragged knits and tattered oversized garments with exposed seams were in stark contrast to the rest of the collections being shown in Paris – with bright colours from Versace and Saint Laurent and figure-hugging sculpted curves from Mugler and Montana – and came as a shock to the Western fashion establishment. Yamamoto pared down his garments to reveal what he called "the beauty that remains when excess has been eliminated" while, with the 1981 Comme des Garçons collection (quickly nicknamed "Le Destroy" by French critics), the innovative Kawakubo struck at Western ideals not only of clothing construction but of beauty – trousers had attached sleeve cuffs, skirts had sleeves hanging from the front of them.

Miyake's approach to fashion, though different, was not as radical or shocking. Miyake begins with the fabric itself and relies on cleverly conceived and often complex construction methods. He experiments with fibres and weaves, and his clothes are often as beautiful when laid flat as when placed on the body. He is famous for his pleated dresses and jackets. He introduced the "Pleats" range in 1988 and the more affordable and machine-washable "Pleats Please" in 1993. In 1999 he added the A-POC range in which an entire outfit is cut out of a single piece of fabric (A-POC stands for "a piece of cloth") and requires no stitching.

The early designs of Rei Kawakubo and Yohji Yamamoto made fashion history and are highly collectable and desirable as are the creations of Kawakubo's one-time protégé Junya Watanabe (born 1961). Issey Miyake's creations do not generally reach the same values so his pleated taffeta dresses are relatively affordable.

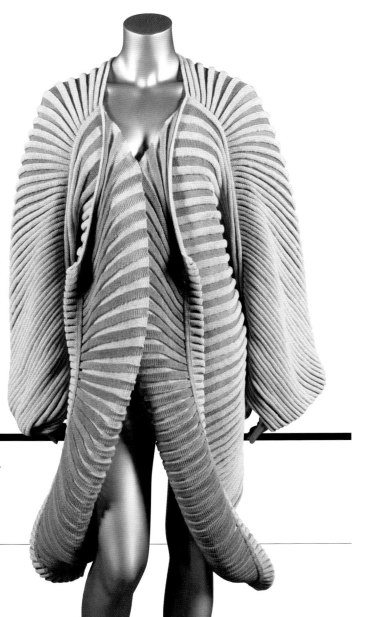

JAPANESE INNOVATION – THE SHOCK OF THE NEW

Opposite left to right, Issey Miyake crinkled and pleated scarlet polyester jacket of voluminous cut and with pointed hood, 1980s. D. Issey Miyake "Shell" coat, 1985, labelled: knitted in cotton, linen and nylon ribs, with curving sleeves. M

Below left to right, Rei Kawakubo/Comme des Garçons printed cotton dress, Spring/Summer 1984. O. Comme des Garçons "beggar" coat, *c.*1982–3: of open-weave wool in black and ivory with floating scarf-like lapel panels that attach at the hem. O

Possibly in reaction to the status-symbol dressing and power suits of the previous decade, the anti-fashion movement known as "grunge" was a mismatched, layered look of denim jackets, granny-style floral dresses, low-waisted thong-revealing jeans, combat trousers, high-waisted shorts, outsized plaid shirts, hoodies, ripped tights, Dr Martens boots, worn-out tennis shoes, and knitted beanie hats or baseball caps, pulled over long, lank, greasy hair. It was an easy and cheap look and is consequently not collectable or desirable today – thank goodness!

The Acid House scene also had its fashions – neon-bright boiler suits (coveralls), white gloves, glow sticks, and baby's dummies. Boy London (which used to peddle punk gear in the 1970s and 1980s) produced brightly coloured club-wear covered in smiley faces and the designers stated that the kids were "sick of wearing black". Anna Sui, Marc Jacobs, and Kansai Yamamoto produced expensive designer versions. Meanwhile, the Spice Girls advocated "girl power" in stretch-Lycra creations and platform trainers that were imitated the world over.

The body-conscious lines of the 1980s continued, but the emphasis moved from the shoulders to a natural, athletic look that defined the physique. Azzedine Alaïa continued producing elegant, clever body-defining clothes; Hervé Léger (who launched his own label in 1993) clothed the torso in a second skin of stretch-Spandex bandages, while sportswear fabrics were increasingly used for high-street fashion. Mugler, Montana, and Antony Price produced curvaceous and glamorous collections. Calvin Klein and Giorgio Armani made stylish, expensive designer label classics.

Italian renaissance

During this decade Italian fashion (already the major centre for mass-producing high-quality ready-to-wear) became especially influential. Moschino, Prada, and Dolce & Gabbana became global brands and the urbane, talented Tom Ford (born 1961) breathed new life into the languishing Gucci. Ford's 1990s eveningwear is sophisticated, elegant, and timeless, and his early pieces for Gucci are already highly collectable.

Moschino (1950–94), renowned for his irreverent approach to the industry, had launched his label in 1983, producing witty, well-tailored suits and cheeky little cocktail dresses. In 1988 he launched his Cheap & Chic line, which exuded all the wit and style of his main line. While highly collectable, Moschino's clothes are relatively affordable despite their creative individuality. The pre-1995 pieces will no doubt increase in value with the passage of time.

Domenico Dolce (born 1958) and Stefano Gabbana (born 1962) opened their first womenswear store in Milan in 1986, before adding swimwear, underwear, and menswear (in 1990). Known for their gangster-style pinstriped women's suits and underwear-as-outerwear looks (something already done by Westwood and Gaultier), their expensive, good-quality but mass-produced clothes are reasonably plentiful and still relatively inexpensive vintage to acquire.

In the late 1970s Miuccia Prada (born 1949) had turned the high-end leather family business (founded 1913) into a leading global luxury brand. Her utilitarian, understated, expensive black nylon waterproof rucksack became the "must-have" designer accessory of the 1990s. In 1992 she introduced the

Introduction

THE POSTMODERN NINETIES

"Every day I'm thinking about change." *Miuccia Prada*

Above, Kate Moss and other
models pose wearing rubber
skirts during the Istante
Versus Versace Spring/
Summer 1995 show.

Miu Miu (her nickname) diffusion line. Her clothes used interesting and unusual modern fabrics such as synthetic organza with beaded adornments, and had refreshingly simple, clean lines. Dropped waistline skirts with broad pleats were easy to wear and stylish. Miuccia Prada designed clothes that she herself would wish to wear and thousands of women agreed with her. Her more lavish creations from the 1990s are probably collectables for the future.

Alexander McQueen produced imaginative, thought-provoking, and beautiful collections working on his own label and also succeeding John Galliano at Givenchy from 1996 to 2001. Anything from McQueen's early collections is coveted – but more so if it is a complete evening ensemble rather than a separate. Fellow Central Saint Martins alumna Stella McCartney (born 1971) graduated in 1995, with Kate Moss and Naomi Campbell modelling her degree show collection as her father Paul looked on with pride.

For his first collection at Christian Dior (Autumn/Winter 1997/98), John Galliano dipped into the archive, with romantic bias-cut creations, fishtail skirts, and layers of lace and tulle that showed off his construction skills and understanding of his new haute couture clientele. It was a sensation. These early "Galliano for Dior" couture pieces are of particular interest to museums and already sell for high sums at auction, as they are both beautiful and historically important.

Left, John Galliano for Christian Dior couture pale lavender lace dress, from his first collection for Dior, Autumn/Winter 1997/98: 1930s-inspired gown cut on the bias with ruffles of lace to the front bodice. N

Left to right, Thierry Mugler rainbow-stripe suit, Spring/Summer 1990: formed from undulating multicoloured bands; asymmetric hem; popper-fastened. K. Two Boy London "Acid House" ensembles featuring "Chanel" smiley-faced motifs and messages, including "If you don't like it ... don't look". Each E

Left to right, Tangerine crêpe and lace "chemise-style" gown, 1997, bearing a "couture" label: the straps with "GV" gilt clasps inset with diamanté, deep flounces of tangerine lace and net to the sides forming a train. K. Bouffant printed silk evening skirt, *c.*1992, "Atelier"-labelled: cut short at the front and cascading in stiffened tiers to the sides; the red bodice with "couture" label. L

GIANNI VERSACE

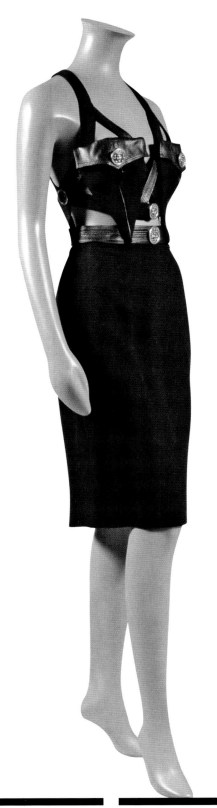

Although his earliest creations date from 1978, Gianni Versace's (1946–97) opulent, in-your-face, and sexy designs really took off in the 1990s. Expensive and showy, he unashamedly admitted that his provocative, brilliantly coloured, and bejewelled creations were inspired by prostitutes. His fashion shows were extravaganzas where supermodels added to the glamour and allure of his brand. Versace understood the importance of celebrity and always ensured that his front row was crammed with stars.

Many of the designs had art-historical influences – Italian Renaissance, Baroque, Etruscan, and Grecian motifs were printed onto luscious satins or rich velvets of the highest quality. He mixed leopard spots with stripes, and floral prints with checks, and created opulent and sensuous metallic-mesh tunics, draped cowl-necked dresses, and outlandish, tiger-striped jumpsuits with mosaic-covered bustier bodices. He loved feather-light, crumpled, floating chiffon, delicate lace, blue denim, and leather (preferably with gold adornments). Underwear as outerwear was important, with little slip-style dresses, delicate skirts of chiffon or lace in a myriad of pastel colours, heavily beaded and jewelled straps, and corset-style front lacing.

For his Spring/Summer 1991 collection, Versace – an art connoisseur – used highly coloured fabrics printed with Warhol images for cocktail suits and full-length evening sheaths, and accompanied them with matching handbags. The Medusa head, beaded onto bustiers and on ornate buckles and printed silks, became synonymous with the Versace brand.

Versace's landmark "Bondage" collection (Autumn/Winter 1992/93) took inspiration from the dominatrix, with gilt-tipped straps and buckles crisscrossed over corset-like bodices in heavy silk jersey with leather details. Although a lot of bare flesh was on show, the interlaced straps made the clothes look and feel highly structured. There were also leather cowboy shirts with gilt-tipped collars and fabulous quilted leather coats with New Look flared skirts. Now seen by museums as must-have fashion benchmarks (that women still love to wear), pieces from this collection are always hotly contested at auction.

Labels from the 1980s are large black and white rectangles. In the 1990s they became smaller and those that declare "Gianni Versace couture" actually aren't. His true couture pieces bear the diamond-shaped "Atelier" labels. In 1993 he launched the Versus diffusion line, with his sister Donatella as head designer.

Versace was tragically murdered in 1997, but Donatella (born 1955) continues the great Versace tradition – a glorious celebration of colour and seduction in dress.

Above, "Bondage" cocktail dress, Autumn/Winter 1992/93, "couture"-labelled. This is one of the most desirable and saleable of all his collections. P

Right, A fine Medusa head beaded and embroidered bodice, *c.*1989–91, "Atelier"-labelled. M. "Gianni Versace couture" label and "Atelier Versace" diamond label – pieces bearing the latter are the nearest to couture.

JEAN PAUL GAULTIER

Having served brief apprenticeships with Pierre Cardin and Michel Goma at Jean Patou, Jean Paul Gaultier (born 1952) exploded onto the Paris fashion scene in 1976. In trademark Breton shirt and tartan kilt, he consistently grabs headlines with his mischievous and androgynous creations.

The corset dress with which his name is synonymous was introduced around 1983 with almost ridiculously pronounced, soft velvet cone-shaped breasts (now rare and thus among the holy grails of fashion finds). His collections, even when seemingly conservative, are always invested with erotic undertones. His Autumn/Winter 1989/90 collection, "Women Against Women", included metallic ensembles with cut-outs for the breasts, open midriffs, and elongated gothic sleeves, all inset with zip fasteners, worn over black fishnet bodies. These are highly coveted, particularly by museums. A long slim skirt with breast-exposing braces for a bodice (Autumn/Winter 1991/92) was famously worn by Madonna at a Gaultier retrospective event in 1992.

Gaultier's varied design references take inspiration from the street, from history, and from "ethnic" sources – ranging from the French can-can (Autumn/Winter 1991/92) to a tribute to Joan of Arc, in which Rastafarian hippies collided with the 18th century (Spring/Summer 1994), and from colourful tattoos and prints (Spring/Summer 1996) to bowling balls (Autumn/Winter 1996/97). "The Long Journey" (Autumn/Winter 1994/95) drew inspiration from China, Tibet, and Mongolia, while Spring/Summer 1998 referenced his admiration for Frieda Kahlo and Latin American culture in general.

Gaultier's beautiful handcrafted haute couture pieces (launched Autumn/Winter 1996/97) bear "Gaultier Paris" labels and demonstrate his talent for luxuriously beautiful eveningwear devoid of brash gimmicks or jokes. Clothes dating from between 1981 and 1994 carry "Gibo" labels, and those between 1995 and 2012 the "Aeffe" label. In 2012 he returned production to Gibo for ready-to-wear. "Gaultier" (replaced in 1994 by the "JPG by Gaultier" unisex collections) and "Junior Gaultier" labels were introduced in 1992 and 1998, respectively.

Above, Model wearing "tattoo" print dress from Gaultier's Spring/Summer 1996 ready-to-wear collection.

Kate Moss's love affair with vintage is well documented and transcends the decades. Moss (born 1974) famously wore an ivory satin, bias-cut thirties gown (mistakenly reported at the time to be Dior), which, when it was ripped, she tied at one hip and wore as a mini with great aplomb. Other memorable vintage ensembles include an early-fifties Jean Dessès cocktail dress of pale yellow draped chiffon (copied for her 2007 Topshop range), a 1970s blue Thea Porter gypsy dress with blue suede boots (worn the night before her wedding to Jamie Hince), and a Vivienne Westwood "Nostalgia of Mud" ("Buffalo Girls") collection toga dress. She declared that her favourite shoes of all time are a pair of well-worn, well-loved "SEX"-labelled shoes from Westwood/McLaren *c.*1976. Simultaneously stylish and slightly alternative, they are a bit like the model herself.

Style Icon

KATE MOSS

"I couldn't really afford designer clothes when I was young, so I just went to second-hand shops. It wasn't called vintage then; it was called second-hand." *Kate Moss in an interview with Women's Wear Daily*

*1920s beaded dresses *1930s bias-cut satin sheath *1940s black monkey-fur jacket *1970s-inspired Biba-style wide-brimmed hat *Skinny jeans *Ballet pumps *1950s Jean Dessès draped chiffon cocktail gown*

Opposite, Moss in a 1992 Philip Treacy hat. Rare Westwood/McLaren black patent "SEX" stilettoes, *c.*1976: the insoles stamped "Especially for SEX, 430 Kings Road, Chelsea, Made in England". N

Above and right, Thea Porter printed muslin hippy-style gown, early 1970s. H. Moss wearing an early 1920s beaded tulle tunic at a film premiere in 1997.

Alexander McQueen (1969–2010) was arguably the greatest designer at the beginning of the 21st century. Born and raised in London, he left school at 16 with one qualification, in art. After a two-year apprenticeship at Anderson & Sheppard (where he reputedly embroidered profanities inside linings of suits made for HRH The Prince of Wales) he moved to Gieves & Hawkes in 1988 where he learned military tailoring. He honed his cutting and tailoring skills on Savile Row, and at renowned film costumiers, Angels, he learnt the construction of historical dress.

After briefly working for avant-garde Japanese designer Kohji Tatsuno, McQueen worked closely with Romeo Gigli in Milan, observing first hand the machinations of a commercial fashion house. Returning to England, he sought employment teaching pattern cutting at Central Saint Martins. So impressed was the lecturer by his portfolio that she offered him a place as a student on their renowned fashion course instead.

His 1992 graduation show, "Jack the Ripper Stalks His Victims", was a sensation – Isabella Blow purchased every piece. At his own label he cut patterns and made the clothes himself with just a couple of helpers – there was no technical requirement that he had not mastered. When working on a collection he would sketch ideas, but also design with fabric straight onto a mannequin or figure. This brilliance, in imaginative design and in his knowledge of construction, sets him apart.

Bumsters

The "bumster", introduced in 1993 and repeated in numerous collections, became one of his signature styles. The very cropped, "bum cleavage"-revealing trouser top elongated the torso and McQueen said: "To me, that part of the body – not so much the buttocks, but the bottom of the spine – that's the most erotic part of anyone's body, man or woman." Naturally this provocative design created headlines and more were to follow.

The dramatic and powerful "Highland Rape" show (Autumn/Winter 1995/96) was shocking at a time when minimalism was the order of the day. Blood-splattered, semi-naked models appeared in bold scarlet McQueen tartan and ripped lace-effect dresses. Referencing his ancestors from the Isle of Skye and "England's rape of Scotland", the collection highlighted a fascination with history and his geneology that continued throughout his career.

Below left, "The Birds" collection jacket, Spring/Summer 1995: of orange gabardine printed in black with swallows in flight; with sharp lapels, massive padded shoulders and painted rubberized finish. McQueen had a keen interest in ornithology. N.

Below and right, Alexander McQueen for Givenchy black crêpe and leopard lace evening gown, Autumn/Winter 1997/98, "couture"-labelled. The more ladylike, less extreme pieces for Givenchy today make less than McQueen's more avant-garde creations. L. "The Overlook" collection, Autumn/Winter 1999/2000.

ALEXANDER McQUEEN

A recluse who refuses to be interviewed or photographed, the Belgian designer Martin Margiela (born 1957) launched his own label in 1988. Dubbed a "deconstructivist", he meticulously reconstructs vintage pieces in new and interesting ways. He is an anti-fashion, yet highly successful fashion designer who has never commissioned advertisements, preferring to show his collections sporadically, often in offbeat locations.

His *défilé* label is a blank piece of white tape with four crude tacking stitches, intentionally featured on the garment's outside. The majority of his labels bear a series of numbers ranging from 0 to 23, with the relevant collection numeral circled: 0 is a unisex, artisanal garment, handmade in small numbers from other clothing; 1 is the main womenswear line; 4 is women's wardrobe (basics); 6 is accessibly priced sportswear; 8 eyewear; 10 menswear; 11 unisex accessories, 12 fine jewellery; 13 objects and publications; 22 shoes for women and men.

For his inaugural Spring/Summer 1989 show, his models wore his (now-signature) Japanese-inspired *Tabi* boots, stepping into red dye before walking along a pristine white-calico catwalk leaving blood-red prints along its length (the fabric was later reused for waistcoats in his Autumn/Winter 1989/90 collection). Based on English tailoring with new shoulder lines that pulled in toward the neck with crescent-shaped padding, there were inside-out jackets and ankle-length waistcoats worn over full-length cotton shirts. Some of his coats came with integral trousers made from lining fabric with drawstring ties to the waist – in this way Margiela could be sure that his "complete look" would be worn as he had envisioned it. Long skirts were made from pairs of trousers with the leg seams cut open and re-sewn flat.

Re-use and recycle

Margiela is famous for recycling everyday materials into clothes of exceptional beauty, such as a bodice made entirely from vintage leather gloves, and he has stated, "It is a nicer feeling for myself to go forward by looking backwards." He also made new reproductions with labels inside stating their provenance (e.g. "boy's shirt, 1970"), and giant replicas of Barbie, Ken, and G.I. Joe clothes for both Autumn/Winter 1994/95 and Spring/Summer 1999. He would copy half of two differing vintage dresses and rejoin them to produce a new "deconstructed" look. For his Spring/Summer 1991 collection, he cut open 1950s layered tulle ball gowns and turned them into tunics worn over old jeans and tank tops. Spring/Summer 1997 took inspiration from tailor's dummies with high-collared calico tunics stencilled with patent numbers.

Margiela manipulates scale, with massive signet ring bracelets and figure-swamping sweaters and jackets. He turns everyday items like paper clips or plastic suit protectors into high fashion and has often reintroduced looks and lines as replica models in later collections. Maison Margiela announced its aim as being "to take an existing form and rework it". Such statements were usually issued using the first personal plural ("we" rather than "I"), suggesting a design collective. Acquired by Diesel in 2002, in December 2009 it was officially announced that Margiela had left the company and Maison Margiela now trades with no named head designer.

It is only the pieces made between 1989 and *c.*2008 (when Margiela was the driving force behind the company) that are currently highly sought after. The mystique, labelling system, and diverse range make this a fascinating collecting area and one that will only increase in interest and value as time passes.

Below left, Tan leather *Tabi* boots, *c.*1990: zip-fastened to the sides; cloven toes. D

Below, Silk jersey bodice and skirt printed overall with sequins, Spring/Summer 1996, blank label (special order or *défilé*). F

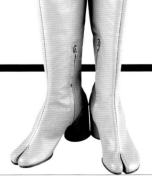

MARTIN MARGIELA

Below left to right, Zipper bodice, *c.*2000, composed of multiple zips in blue, brown and wine shades. J. Martin Margiela Semi Couture bodice in imitation of a tailor's dummy, 1996: the tan toile-effect exterior stamped "Semi Couture, Paris, Brevete". L

Right, Martin Margiela unisex, artisanal label

Outside fashion's mainstream there were a number of nonconformist designers who regarded fashion as an applied art and often displayed their clothing in modern art settings – the Belgian Martin Margiela, Dries Van Noten, and Ann Demeulemeester; the Japanese Yohji Yamamoto, Issey Miyake, Rei Kawakubo, and Junya Watanabe; the Dutch Viktor & Rolf, and the Cypriot-born British-trained designer Hussein Chalayan.

Regarded as one of the greatest designers of the 20th century, Yohji Yamamoto became an independent designer on graduating in 1969. Highly respected in his native Japan, he became internationally known in 1981, when he showed in Paris at the same time as Rei Kawakubo. His Autumn/Winter 1991/92 dresses formed from wooden panelling on black felt were akin to major sculpture. It is this challenging, fresh approach to design, eschewing preconceived ideas, that makes him one of the greats.

Yamamoto's complex, contorted, twisted, knotted, and deconstructed clothes (it can be a challenge deciphering front from back) of the 1990s are highly desirable. His exquisite Spring/Summer 1998 satin evening gowns with twisted straps and bands coiled round the body were reminiscent of 1930s Grecian goddess-style creations, and use no cuts or darts to create the sensuous shape.

Other major themes in Yamamoto's work are his use of traditional Japanese workwear and of European historic fashions, including the bustle-backed dress and 19th-century "Visite" jacket. He relishes back details, stating, "The back supports the clothes, and so if it is not properly made, the front cannot exist." His clothes, almost sculptural in their monotone simplicity, have a minimal beauty, focusing the eye on shape and proportion. He is regarded as a grand master of cut and

Below, Comme des Garçons ivory tousled knit tunic dress, probably early 1990s: with wide, scooped neck and irregular collar; the knitted ground looped and embroidered with cotton-wool cords. M

construction, and his cerebral approach to fashion attracts many admirers. Yamamoto is one of the most desirable and valuable of the major Japanese designers.

Junya Watanabe worked at Comme des Garçons after graduating in 1984. Introducing his own label for the brand in 1992, he is regarded as the heir apparent to the company's founder, Rei Kawakubo. Unlike the traditional monochrome palette used by many Japanese designers, Watanabe revels in colour as well as texture. In the early 1990s he used acid-coloured PVC, followed by black leather and jewel-coloured brocades. Traditional men's suitings combined with Japanese floral weaves for highly feminine clothing with a masculine severity. His Autumn/Winter 1998/99 collection combined plain cotton shirt-dresses with crinoline-like, wire-hemmed, green serge skirts. His work demonstrates his skill in traditional cutting techniques and love of high-tech modern fabrics. He is one of the most desirable and innovative of the Japanese "deconstructivist" or conceptual designers, and his iconic creations are some of the most prized and sought after, alongside those of his mentor, Rei Kawakubo.

"Hyères" (Autumn/Winter 1993), the first show of Viktor Horsting and Rolf Snoeren (both born 1969), was based on distortion, deconstruction, and layering, with large bell-shaped tattered and torn skirts, asymmetric jackets and trousers. The duo first showed haute couture in Paris (Spring/Summer 1998) with models standing on plinths like statues, wearing layered, draped, and origami-style creations, with wired winged collars, bubbled and ruffled collars, and plain black columns gathered around the face. "Atomic Bomb" (Autumn/Winter 1998/99 haute couture) featured massive mushroom-cloud, cushioned

CONCEPTUAL FASHION

"The people who buy my clothes take fashion seriously. They get a kick out of wearing something new. These are the people I design for. I'm not interested in the mainstream." *Junya Watanabe*

collars, giant pom-pom collars, harlequinade prints, and plain black garments with accents of brilliant colour. "Blacklight" (Spring/Summer 1999) saw black tuxedos appliquéd with white silk ribbon skeletons or with oversized ruffled white collars from which the head barely emerged, flamenco-style skirts, and ruffled edges on trousers and sleeves. "Russian Doll" (Autumn/Winter 1999/2000) was a piece of performance art in which a gamine model on a turntable overlaid a simple raw-edged gauze shift with a succession of garments – a lace appliquéd cocktail dress with beaded trim and bow; a long shimmering silver-mesh dress with wide shoulders; rich brocaded lamé and bejewelled full-length gowns, and further layers – until only the top of the head was visible at the back and the face was cocooned in a cone-like cape with a massive rose to one shoulder. Although important, Viktor & Rolf have yet to sell for significant sums at auction.

Hussein Chalayan (born 1970) buried his graduate collection, "The Tangent Flows" (1993) in a friend's garden for six months before exhuming the partly decomposed garments for display on the catwalk. It was bought in its entirety by Browns, London. Regarded as a visionary, he was described by *Vogue* as "Fashion's arch avant-gardist". With his innovative use of materials and modern technology, and his architectural approach, his work (such as a wooden, coffee-table skirt or LED dresses) is sometimes deemed unwearable and uncommercial. These eccentric but beautiful creations may grab the headlines, but the clean, structured, geometric lines of his ready-to-wear collection are equally outstanding. His more avant-garde creations are highly desirable but rarely come onto the market.

Left, Hussein Chalayan
Spring/Summer 2000
collection.

Right, Junya Watanabe for Comme des Garçons suit, 1996, labelled: the fabric is an interesting mixture of traditional Japanese print and finely woven Prince of Wales checked wool. L

Fashion may change but style is eternal. As a new century begins, eager young designers step forward to take the place of the great names of the past.

Looking back over a century of trends we have seen everything from S-shaped corsetry and voluptuous décolletages to boyishly flat chests; flowing, full-length skirts to miniskirts and hot pants; figure-hugging bias-cut gowns to dresses made of plastic, wood, or paper, and dresses you can wear upside down or inside out... Where do we go next?

Rise of the designer label

The second half of the 20th century saw a move toward expensive high-fashion ready-to-wear, with corporate branding and high-end advertising and packaging. Cosmetics, perfume, and accessories are now the main money spinners for a fashion house.

Designer label boutiques and ready-to-wear lines have all but eclipsed haute couture, originally the *raison d'être* of all major fashion houses. Some ready-to-wear lines proudly display "couture" labels but, of course, aren't. Because elaborate ready-to-wear pieces by fashion houses such as Alexander McQueen can cost five figures and a boutique suit by Chanel the same as a small car, the line between couture and ready-to-wear has been blurred. These pricey modern garments make buying vintage not only a sound investment but also something of a bargain.

Collecting 21st-century fashion

Contemporary or near-contemporary designers and fashion houses who have already sold successfully at auction (including Nicolas Ghesquière, John Galliano, Rei Kawakubo, Junya Watanabe, Yohji Yamamoto, Issey Miyake, and Azzedine Alaïa) will probably continue to do so. Stella McCartney, Roland Mouret, recent Chanel, Tom Ford for Gucci, and Ford's independent 2010 womenswear collection are especially popular with buy-to-wear clients.

The untimely death of Alexander McQueen robbed the world of a design genius but new young talent is emerging. Ones to watch include Gareth Pugh, Christopher Kane, Sarah Burton for McQueen, Mary Katrantzou, Raf Simons for Dior, Haider Ackermann (whom Lagerfeld once named as a possible successor), Riccardo Tisci for Givenchy, Phoebe Philo for Chloé and Longchamp, and Marc Jacobs for Louis Vuitton.

Sedate, classic ensembles by good designers, although eminently wearable, are unlikely to become major collectables. It is the outrageous, ground-breaking pieces or fabulous, romantic ball gowns and eveningwear that people clamour for, rather than prim little day suits, whoever designed them. Show-stopping, jaw-dropping fashion is what buyers demand – be it for the red carpet or the museum exhibit.

The other noticeable growth area has been the designer handbag. Although the market is led by Hermès, closely followed by Chanel and Gucci, it is probable that other brands will follow. The classic Hermès Birkin, Kelly, and Constance bags and the Chanel 2.55 in black leather are the most prized. The most desirable Gucci bag is a 1960s example with curved bamboo handle. Other modern expensive designer bags may not be a good investment in the short term, but may retain or even slightly increase in value in the future.

Below, Nicolas Ghesquière for Balenciaga evening coat, 2005: with curved hips and narrow elastane waistband; the cuffs and hem adorned with gold sequins. Ghesquière is one of the great talents of the 21st century. Q

Introduction

THE NEW CENTURY

"Clothes mean nothing until someone lives in them." *Marc Jacobs*

Right, Mary Katrantzou, Spring/Summer 2013, featuring imaginative prints based on Venezuelan stamps and bank notes.

After eight seasons of showing independently, McQueen signed for Givenchy in Paris in 1996. He committed to two haute couture and two ready-to-wear collections annually, while simultaneously continuing his own label collections. This working-class East Ender was now head of the soignée Parisian house.

During McQueen's tenure at Givenchy (1996–2001), working with the highly skilled *petites mains*, using the best fabrics, and learning couture finishes were a revelation to him. But sharp tailoring, pronounced shoulder features, and accentuated waists remained hallmarks – many of his clothes have integral corsets to hold the figure correctly in place. With its wide shoulders and nipped-in waists, his Autumn/Winter 2009/10 collection "The Horn of Plenty" was particularly influenced by couture of the 1950s.

In 2001 the designer sold 51 percent of Alexander McQueen to the Gucci group, which gave him the financial backing he needed to fund his ever-more imaginative shows and collections. Love and beauty, dark and light, aggressor and victim, nature, ornithology, his ancestral history, historicism, tribal and folk traditions, were all interwoven to produce collections and shows of breathtaking beauty and originality, more

Below left to right, Bugle-beaded evening gown, "In memory of Elizabeth Howe, Salem 1692", ready-to-wear collection, Autumn/Winter 2007/08. Elizabeth Howe was an ancestor of McQueen who was burned as a witch in Salem in the 17th century. W. "Plato's Atlantis" collection snakeskin-printed organza dress, Spring/Summer 2010: with python-like photo-collage print in brilliant colours. "Plato's Atlantis" was McQueen's final completed collection. U

LATER McQUEEN

"Everything I do is based on tailoring."
Alexander McQueen

Above and right, Autumn/Winter 2009/10 ready-to-wear, in which McQueen played with proportions – using giant houndstooth checks in a Dior-esque parody. Checked coats, dresses, tights, shoes, and gloves were printed with the check in contrasting sizes. Black and gold damask evening jacket, 2006. J

"Working in the atelier (at Givenchy) was fundamental to my career ... Because I was a tailor, I didn't totally understand softness, or lightness. I learned lightness at Givenchy. I was a tailor at Savile Row. At Givenchy I learned to soften. For me, it was an education." *Alexander McQueen*

Left, Aran knit evening dress, "The Horn of Plenty" collection, Autumn/Winter 2009/10, incorporating chunky-knit covered tyre "necklaces" and hem. S

Below and right, Harlequin-print organza cocktail gown, also "The Horn of Plenty". In this piece McQueen reveals his total mastery of construction. V. Red and black ostrich feather and glass medical slide-dress, "Voss" collection, Spring/Summer 2001.

akin to performance art than commercial catwalk show. Hats made in collaboration with Philip Treacy and Dai Rees, and jewellery made with Shaun Leane, Erik Halley, and Sarah Harmarnee, completed the dramatic McQueen look.

McQueen's boyhood interests of swimming and ornithology created constant design sources for collections including "Voss", "Irere", and "It's a Jungle Out There", in which deer antlers burst from the shoulders of his garments. For "Plato's Atlantis" (Spring/ Summer 2010), he imagined a flooded world where life on earth has evolved to exist below the water. Digitally printed and woven fabrics featured a kaleidoscopic mixture of reptile and feather prints in vivid colours. Not only was the print extraordinary, so was the woven damask satin organza and chiffon onto which it was placed. The gowns were created by draping and pinning the fabric straight onto the form and accessorized by vertiginous armadillo claw-like shoes. The show was streamed live over the Internet to a global audience and McQueen said, "There is no way back for me now. I am going to take you on journeys you've never dreamed were possible."

McQueen was working on a collection portentously named "Angels & Demons" (Autumn/Winter 2010/11) when he died. Eighty percent complete, it was finished by his assistant and successor, Sarah Burton (born 1974). Sixteen magical pieces conceived around the themes of good and evil, heaven and hell, showed inspiration from Flemish paintings, heraldry, and Gothic works of art. Specially commissioned fabrics included jacquard-weave silks depicting Hieronymus Bosch demons, heraldic beasts, and gilded angels. Shimmering gold embroidery and feathers contrasted with muted brown silk damask and soft ivory tulle layers. Sarah Burton described McQueen working on this collection thus: "He wanted to get back to the handcraft he loved, and the things that are being lost in the making of fashion. He was looking at the art of the Dark Ages but finding light and beauty in it."

The Honourable Daphne Guinness (born 1967) is a 21st-century style icon with her signature black and blonde coiffure, elegant couture wardrobe, extravagant accessories, and jewellery. She began her collection with Alaïa and her first couture was a Lacroix cocktail dress with puffball skirt. Guinness regularly wears vintage fashion, appreciating the design of the couturiers and their skill and craftsmanship, both today and in times past.

Guinness must delight contemporary designers because, while couture clients often have conservative tastes, she wears their more outrageous pieces. She is also not afraid to mix high street with haute couture, or combine pieces from previous decades, with no qualms about wearing a sequined Chanel cocktail dress with an Alaïa cutwork leather belt, or a 1930s ostrich feather cape over a modern Valentino couture evening gown with a Philip Treacy hat or items from Claire's Accessories. It is this skill in assembling something new that sets her apart. Her wardrobe is akin to a glorious dressing-up box with Mainbocher, Schiaparelli, Madame Grès, Christian Dior, and Balenciaga among her favourites.

She favours black, teaming it with a crisp white high-collared shirt and towering elevated wedge, stiletto, or platform shoes. By night she becomes a creature of fantasy. She could be wearing a vintage couture bias-cut piece from the 1930s, a Balenciaga magenta faille tent coat from the 1950s, or a fabulous Alexander McQueen creation of recent years. Her accessories and jewellery will be chosen for maximum impact – hats by Philip Treacy, boots by Hogan McLaughlin, shoes by Natacha Marro, Noritaka Tatehana, and body-armour-like jewellery by Shaun Leane.

Left and right, Guinness at Alexander McQueen's memorial service. Guinness in 2010, wearing a jacket of her own design, a dress by McQueen and blue-glitter heel-less platform shoes by Massaro. *Below right,* Alexander McQueen evening dress, 2004: with "string vest" bodice, appliquéd with jungle camouflage foliage over layers of nude chiffon. L

Style Icon

DAPHNE GUINNESS

"Daphne is one of – if not the – most stylish women living. Her style is completely unique and often eccentric, but her keen understanding of her looks, her body, and most importantly her character and personality, make everything that she wears feel as though it has been made for her – and, of course, in many instances it has." *Tom Ford on Guinness*

What would Daphne wear?

*Towering shoes *A white shirt of her own design by day *Graphic black and white combinations *Vintage Balenciaga or Dior evening gowns with armour-like jewellery by night

Basic tips

There are three distinct types of collectors – buy-to-wear; collectors (including private collectors, fashion historians, and museums), who see vintage fashion as an important decorative art and would never dream of wearing a piece; and designers looking for inspiration. The following guidelines will have varying importance according to which group you belong to:

First and foremost, only buy something that you love.

Markets go up and down – if you really like the piece, when the price goes up it's a bonus; when it goes down, you still have something you like.

For buy-to-wear pieces, check the condition.

Don't buy something that will disintegrate on the first outing. Sometimes the threads on the seams have rotted from poor-quality dry-cleaning solutions or from age. This is not serious because seams can be re-sewn – though it can be embarrassing if your dress slowly starts, quite literally, to come apart at the seams (as I know to my own cost)! More serious are splits and tears in the fabric itself, which are costly and sometimes impossible to repair well. Edwardian silks tend to have rotted due to the tin washes used to give them a better, sleeker feel, so do take care if buying antique dress items. Heavily beaded 1920s dresses can also be problematic if they haven't been properly cared for – the weight of the beads can tear a dress apart if it has been left on a hanger for any length of time. If you are buying a 1920s flapper dress to wear, it's better to purchase a *prêt-à-porter* piece, with beads applied to a sturdy muslin ground rather than a silk or chiffon ground. Look for moth holes by holding the dress or fabric against the light. This also helps highlight small darned repairs that you might otherwise have missed.

Try to get something that actually fits you.

If the garment requires drastic alterations, be aware that alterations will cause the piece to lose most of its value. If it's too big and you *must* take it in, try as much as possible to refrain from cutting the fabric. If it's too small, do not tell yourself you will diet to fit it – this rarely happens in reality!

For investment pieces, condition is also crucial.

Underarm stains and other stains generally drastically devalue a piece, as do serious alterations. Expensive dresses were often reused or passed on to another generation and so waists were commonly let in and out and hems went up and down. A garment without alterations is best, though a minor waistline adjustment may be forgivable. However, once a pair of scissors has been applied to a gown, you have probably lost the majority of the value. For example, a superb ball gown by a master of construction such as Balenciaga might be worth about £3000 ($5000) if perfect, but more like £300 ($500) if seriously altered. Some of my clients are perplexed to see that I spend more time forensically examining the inside of a dress than looking at the outside!

When looking for labels, look inside the waist seams, bodice side seams, and skirt seams.

Depending on the designer and the period, they are concealed in a variety of places. If the dress is semi transparent, the couture label was usually just added to the petticoat – so check there as well.

Below, Black velvet Chanel earrings, 1980s. B

COLLECTING VINTAGE

Below, Elsa Schiaparelli couture "Persian Prince"-embroidered black wool evening coat, Autumn/Winter 1937/38; labelled "Schiaparelli London". O

Vintage markets

Bringing together a host of smaller traders, these are a happy hunting ground for those in search of that elusive bargain and are usually wide-ranging in terms of content and price. Britain, France, and the US have thriving vintage markets, usually held over a weekend, with hundreds of stallholders. London's monthly "Frock Me!", held at Chelsea Town Hall (on the King's Road), is one of the best known, with other major fairs held at Hammersmith Town Hall (King Street) and Goodwood House in West Sussex. Brimfield in Massachusetts is arguably the largest flea market in the US with more than 2000 general antiques stallholders including a strong section of vintage clothing, while Manhattan Vintage is held each October, February, and April in New York (West 18th Street). The Salon du Vintage in Paris (Espace d'animation des Blancs Manteaux, 48 rue Vieille du Temple) is held twice yearly and attracts tens of thousands of visitors. Florence, Italy hosts a large specialist vintage fair, usually in January.

Vintage shops

These are popping up internationally and range from small traders in local towns right up to internationally renowned dealers who count film stars and major celebrities among their clientele. Examples include:

London: Rellik (8 Golborne Road, Notting Hill), Virginia (98 Portland Road, Holland Park), and William Vintage (2 Marylebone Street)

Los Angeles: Lily et Cie (9044 Burton Way, Beverly Hills), Decades (8214 Melrose Avenue), and Resurrection (8006 Melrose Avenue)

New York City: Rare Vintage (24 West 57th Street) and New York Vintage (117 West 25th Street)

Paris: Scarlett Vintage (3 rue Chambiges, 8 arr.) and Didier Ludot (26 Galerie Montpensier, 1 arr.)

By visiting a vintage store, you can try the pieces on, receive personal attention, and free advice. The store can provide alteration services and payment plans.

Online

This is a massive global market, from eBay to specialist online vintage dealers. When you buy, ensure that you get precise condition reports and measurements. Pay by credit card or PayPal to ensure that you have some comeback if the goods are not as described.

By auction

Most auctioneers guarantee their lots for authenticity, but check their conditions of business. It's an exciting way to buy and a great way to build up your knowledge, because you can browse online or in person. Importantly, you can check which things sell, which don't, and which pieces go through the roof. Markets change constantly: at one moment Ossie Clark may be flavour of the month; the next sale he's out and maybe Pucci is in. So *when* you buy can affect *how much* you pay. Big museum exhibitions or specialist book releases featuring a particular designer can also cause prices to escalate. You can usually bid in person (great fun if you like it), online, by telephone, or by written bid. Condition reports and size details are provided pre-sale and most good auction houses provide help with shipping. The UK, the US, and France all have specialist auctioneers in this field including:

UK: Kerry Taylor Auctions (up to seven specialist auctions per year), Christie's London (usually one auction per year)

USA: Augusta Auctions, Charles A. Whitaker Auction Company, Leslie Hindman Auctioneers

France: Paris-based experts Chombert Sternbach and Pénélope Blanckaert all work with a variety of auctioneers to produce numerous high-quality and entertaining auctions every year

WHERE TO BUY

Buyer beware! Vintage fakes and forgeries

Not everything bearing an haute couture label is haute couture. Make sure that the label and the style of the label is correct for the dress in terms of its construction and also for the date of the piece. A label added to a garment can alter the value from maybe the low hundreds to the thousands or even tens of thousands – and so, unfortunately, this practice has become widespread in recent years. For instance, punk clothing made by Boy in the 1980s using Westwood original patterns can have the Boy labelling removed and Seditionaries labels added, which increases the value dramatically.

Modern fake garments have also been made with either reproduction labels or genuine labels then added. In recent years, high prices have been paid for both fine haute couture and Westwood/McLaren punk pieces and this has attracted a new form of fraudster making brand-new garments to cash in. The market for Seditionaries T-shirts has plummeted due to the modern (not even Boy) fakes flooding the market on an almost industrial scale. These T-shirts are tempting to fraudsters because they are relatively easy to make and cheap to produce – the originals are simple stencils or screen prints on cotton jersey.

Worrying trends for haute couture fakes have recently been seen in Paris, where there are still skilled couture cutters and finishers capable of recreating couture creations from past decades. A green satin bias-cut dress with an Augustabernard label recently turned up: the construction was correct, the finishing was all hand-locked, but the fabric looked brand new. Hidden in a side seam was a selvedge edge printed "100% *soie*" (100% silk) – something that simply wasn't done in the 1930s when the dress was supposed to have been made. Since then numerous examples have come onto the market, all brand-new, beautifully hand-finished, couture-standard-style evening gowns bearing top French couture labels such as Vionnet, Louise Boulanger, and Augustabernard – though any top French name can be used. These historically correct but modern dresses have probably been made using a poor-condition original gown from which the pattern or toile has been taken. The old couture label is then reapplied to the now seemingly mint-condition vintage gown! These are *not* over-ambitious restoration jobs, but cynical attempts to deceive. Although probably originating in Paris, they have infiltrated markets the world over – so don't feel secure just because you are buying in other countries.

Look at the fabric in detail. Is it aged? Does it show real signs of wear? Does the label have the same amount of wear as the garment itself – or does it look much older? Is the label soiled to the same degree as the garment? Is the label sewn into the correct place in the dress? For example – if a 1920s dress has a large couture label (rather than a *prêt-à-porter* "Made in France" label, which is okay) sewn into the neck, then be suspicious. Couture labels are usually applied to the waist seam, bodice, or skirt side seams – rarely, if ever, at the neck, where they would have been uncomfortable or cumbersome.

Handbags are another highly popular area for forgeries – Chanel, Hermès, and Louis Vuitton being favourite targets. It is part of the Hermès marketing strategy that, if you want to buy the status-symbol Birkin model, you have to put your name on a waiting list, so Chinese factories are more than happy to supply the demand at a fraction of the cost. While these may be pretty convincing at first glance, inspection of the finer details of craftsmanship soon reveals what's what. Most auctioneers guarantee their wares, but if you are buying from a dealer or online, request to see the original sales receipt. Chanel has tried to protect its wares with holograms, plastic ID cards, and ID numbers, but these, too, are also now being faked.

Finally, if the bag is made from an endangered species skin such as crocodile, ask to see the original CITES licence. Bags made from exotic leathers post-1976 are required to have proof that the animal has not been taken from the wild and should have been supplied with a CITES licence to prove it.

VINTAGE FORGERIES

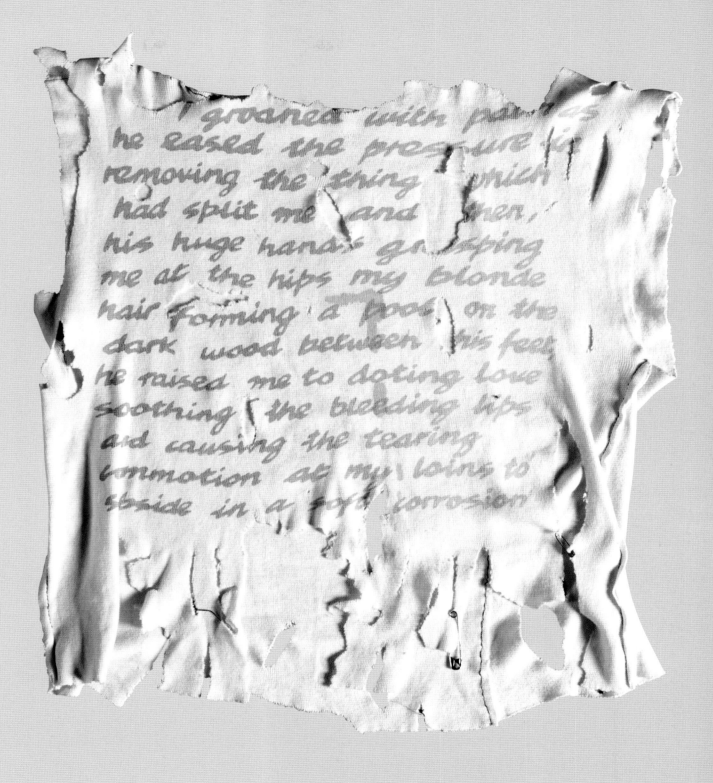

I groaned with pain as
he eased the pressure
removing the thing which
had split me and then,
his huge hands grasping
me at the hips my blonde
hair forming a pool on the
dark wood between his feet
he raised me to doting love
soothing the bleeding lips
and causing the tearing
commotion at my loins to
abide in a soft corrosion

Never use wire coat hangers.
They are responsible for wrecking so many beautiful clothes. The narrow wire span cuts into shoulders if left for any length of time. Use padded hangers or wooden ones which give more support.

Don't hang beaded or heavy garments.
Store any important couture or heavily ornamented pieces flat. Acid-free tissue paper should be folded within the garment and compressed folds should be avoided by using paper rolls of tissue to form a bolster.

Keep clothes out of direct light.
It will inevitably cause fading. It is particularly common to see terrible bleach marks on purple or blue garments along fold lines or sleeves where they have been partially exposed.

Choose your dry cleaner carefully.
The most expensive are not necessarily the best, use personal recommendations. Ask your local theatre company or museum who they use for richly embroidered or couture pieces. Some marks such as underarm perspiration stains simply won't come out, so you may waste money trying. Ask the proprietor if they think that they can really make an improvement before you have the work done.

Wear with care.
Try not to put your heel through the hem. As obvious as this may seem, it is the most commonly found form of damage to dresses (the second being tears at the underarms).

Don't keep fur in plastic suit carriers.
This will cause it to moult and possibly also dry out.

Most vintage pieces don't come with care labels!
If you decide to hand wash a garment, test a corner carefully to see if it causes dye-run or shrinkage. Never wash anything with sequins (frequently made of gelatin in the thirties, which will dissolve in water). Dry cleaners should test before attempting to clean. All but the most experienced and knowledgeable will not be able to deal with them.

TAKING CARE OF YOUR COLLECTION

One final warning.

Don't stand near fires or hot photographic lights wearing 1920s–30s sequined garments – they will melt!

A word on moths.

Moths are one of the biggest threats to any vintage collector. They love dark, slightly humid conditions, where they can breed and chomp their way through priceless textiles. New pesticide regulations now exclude some of the best chemicals for killing the moth, so many domestic sprays are no longer very effective. Here are a few tips to help you preserve your precious vintage garments:

– Always check new pieces for infestation.
– Never store away soiled clothing. Moths love perspiration, so inspect underarms etc. for activity.

– Get moth traps (small cardboard wigwams with a pheromone capsule and sticky coating). They will not kill all of the moths but will alert you to infestation hot spots so you can tackle them properly. Once you discover a problem, you need to treat the clothes immediately – place them (where practical) within a plastic covering and deep-freeze for at least a week. Dry cleaning also kills the moth, but alert your dry cleaner to the problem first.

– With serious infestations, where moths have infiltrated carpets, furniture, and clothes, use a mixture of fumigation and heat treatment. Commercial companies have specially built chambers that heat furniture and textiles at a constant low temperature that kills the insects, larvae, and eggs. They charge by volume.

– Moths hate light and movement, so regularly inspect your wardrobes and drawers and take the pieces out. As a precaution, place anything made of wool or heavy silk in zippered plastic clothes carriers. Apart from wool (and they love natural dyes), moths are attracted to anything with fur or feathers, so be particularly vigilant about checking these over and keep them in zippered fabric covers so that, if you do have an attack, they cannot easily decimate the rest of your wardrobe.

– Sandalwood balls, lavender, etc. smell nice but are a complete waste of money. In your war against the moth, be vigilant, pounce on the slightest sign, and keep monitoring!

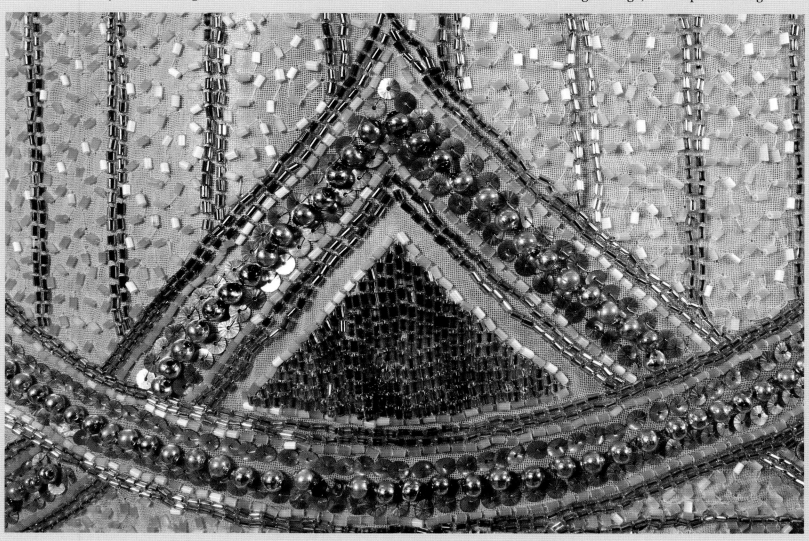

Balenciaga, in interview with Prudence Glynn, "Interview with Cristóbal Balenciaga", *The Times*, August 1971 [page 6/quoted on page 85]

Bettina Ballard, *In My Fashion* (Philadelphia, PA: David McKay Publications, 1960) [page 231/quoted on page 70]

Pierre Balmain, *My Years and Seasons* (London: Cassell, 1964) [page 177/quoted on page 80]

Celia Birtwell, *Celia Birtwell* (London: Quadrille, 2011)

Tim Blanks, "The Transformer", *Vogue* (December 2006) [quoted on page 199]

Dilys E Blum, *Shocking! The Art and Fashion of Elsa Schiaparelli* (Philadelphia: The Philadelphia Museum of Art, 2003)

Marc Bohan, in conversation with the author [quoted on page 50]

Andrew Bolton, *Alexander McQueen: Savage Beauty* (New York: The Metropolitan Museum of Art, 2011)

Danièle Bott, *Thierry Mugler: Galaxy Glamour* (London: Thames and Hudson, 2010) [pages 136 and 160/Mugler quoted on page 165]

Richard Buckle (ed), *Self-Portrait with Friends: The Selected Diaries of Cecil Beaton, 1926–1974* (London: Weidenfeld & Nicolson) [page 151/quoted on page 61]

Elizabeth Ann Coleman, *The Opulent Era: Fashions of Worth, Doucet and Pingat* (New York: The Brooklyn Museum, 1989)

Claude Deloffre (ed), *Thierry Mugler: Fashion, Fetish, Fantasy* (General Publishing Group, 1998)

Amalia Descalzo, Pierre Arizzoli-Clémentel and Miren Arzalluz, *Balenciaga* (Getaria: Cristóbal Balenciaga Museoa, 2011)

Christian Dior, translated by Antonia Fraser, *Dior by Dior: The Autobiography of Christian Dior* (London: V&A Publications, 2007) [page 21/quoted on page 70]

Rudy Gernreich, American *Vogue* (1965) [quoted on page 121]

Rudy Gernreich, *Women's Wear Daily* (1962) [quoted on page 121]

Francoise Giroud, *Dior* (London: Thames and Hudson, 1987)

Pamela Golbin (ed.), *Madeleine Vionnet* (New York: Rizzoli) [Vionnet quoted on page 52]

Lady Duff Gordon, *Discretions & Indiscretions* (London: Frederick A. Stokes, 1932) [quoted on page 19]

Paul Gorman, *The Look: Adventures in Rock & Pop Fashion* (London: Adelita, 2006)

Groninger Museum, *Alaïa: Azzedine Alaïa in the 21st Century* (Groningen: Groninger Museum, 2012) [Alaïa quoted on page 171]

Ernest Hemingway, *Fiesta: The Sun Also Rises* (London: Arrow, 1926) [quoted on page 36]

Georgina Howell (ed), *In Vogue: Six Decades of Fashion*, (New York: Viking, 1975)

Laura Jacobs, "Grace Kelly's Forever Look", *Vanity Fair* May 2010 [Laura Clark quoted on page 86]

Bianca Jagger in conversation with Francisco Costa, *Harper's Bazaar* (October 2011) [quoted on page 146]

Catherine Join-Dieterle, *Givenchy: 40 Years of Creation*, exh. cat. (Paris: Paris-Musées, 1991) [Givenchy quoted on page 117]

Marie-Andrée Jouve and Jacqueline Demornex, *Balenciaga* (New York: 1989) [page 96/Coco Chanel quoted on page 83]

Pamela Clarke Keogh, *Audrey Style* (London: Arum Press, 2009) [Edith Head quoted on page 118]

Betty Kirke, *Madeleine Vionnet* (London: Chronicle Books, 1998) [page 14/Vionnet quoted on page 52]

Harold Koda and Andrew Bolton, *Chanel* (New York: The Metropolitan Museum of Art, 2005) [Coco Chanel quoted on page 37]

Harold Koda and Andrew Bolton, *Poiret* (New York: The Metropolitan Museum of Art, 2007)

Harold Koda and Andrew Bolton, *Schiaparelli and Prada: Impossible Conversations* (New York: The Metropolitan Museum of Art, 2012) [Schiaparelli quoted on page 46]

Joanna Lumley, in conversation with the author [quoted on page 144]

Martin Margiela, Interview with Suzy Menkes in *The New York Times*, 6 September 1994. [quoted on page 196]

Colin McDowell, *Galliano* (London: Orion, 1998)

Colin McDowell, *Jean Paul Gaultier* (New York: Viking Studio, 2001)

Deirdre McSharry, *Daily Express*, 23 February 1966 [quoted on page 108]

Valerie D Mendes and Amy de la Haye, *Lucile Ltd: London, Paris, New York and Chicago 1890s–1930s* (London: V&A Publications, 2009)

Caroline Reynolds Millbank, *New York Fashion: The Evolution of American Style* (New York: Harry N Abrams, 1989) [page 146/Adrian quoted on page 66]

Peggy Moffitt and William Claxton, *The Rudi Gernreich Book* (New York: Rizzoli, 1991)

Kate Moss, in interview with Brid Costello, "Kate Moss on Vintage, Perfume, Style and Life", *Women's Wear Daily* (13th November 2009) [quoted on page 192]

Jane Mulvagh, *Vivienne Westwood: An Unfashionable Life* (London: Harper Collins, 1999)

Guillermo de Osma, *Mariano Fortuny: His Life and Work* (London: Arum Press, 1980)

BIBLIOGRAPHY

Marie-Paule Pellé and Patrick Mauriès, *Valentino's Magic*, revised edn. (New York: Abbeville Press, 1998)

Paul Poiret, translated by Stephen Haden Guest, *King of Fashion: The Autobiography of Paul Poiret* (London: V&A Publications, 2009)

Paul Poiret, *My First Fifty Years* (London: Victor Gollanz, 1931) [page 36/quoted on page 17]

Brenda Polan and Roger Tredre, *The Great Fashion Designers* (London: Berg, 2009) [Issey Miyake quoted on page 52]

Mary Quant, *Quant by Quant: The Autobiography of Mary Quant* (London: V&A Publications, 2012)

Elsa Schiaparelli, *Shocking Life: The Autobiography of Elsa Schiaparelli* (London: V&A Publications, 2007) [page 46/quoted on page 46. Page 107/quoted on page 63]

Anne Sebba, *That Woman: The Life of Wallis Simpson, Duchess of Windsor* (London: Phoenix, 2012) [Wallis Simpson quoted on page 50]

Eugenia Shepherd, *The New York Times* (1971) [quoted on page 135]

Ginette Spanier, *It Isn't All Mink* (London: Collins, 1959) [page 179/quoted on page 81]

Stevie Stewart, in conversation with the author [quoted on page 163]

Alwyn W Turner, *The Biba Experience* (Antique Collectors' Club)

American *Vogue*, 1926 [quoted on page 38]

American *Vogue*, 1 September 1940. [quoted on page 65]

Diana Vreeland, *D.V* (New York: Ecco Press, 2011) [page 139/quoted on page 84]

Junya Watanabe, in interview with Susannah Frankel in *Dazed & Confused*, January 2003 [quoted on page 198]

Judith Watt, *Ossie Clark, 1965–74* (London: V&A Publications)

Iain R Webb, *Bill Gibb: Fashion and Fantasy* (London: V&A Publications, 2008)

Iain R Webb, *Foale and Tuffin: The Sixties A Decade in Fashion* (ACC Editions, 2009)

Belle Whitney, *Damerini* page 90 [quoted on page 21]

Claire Wilcox (ed), *The Golden Age of Couture: Paris and London 1947–57* (London: V&A Publications, 2007) [page 42/Carmel Snow quoted on page 70. Dior quoted on page 76]

Claire Wilcox, *Vivienne Westwood* (London: V&A Publications, 2004)

C. Willet-Cunnington, *English Women's Clothing in the Present Century* (London: Faber and Faber, 1952), [page 216/unknown magazine quoted on page 44. Page 239/*Vogue* quoted on page 42]

Mark Wilson, *Alaïa: Azzedine Alaïa in the 21st Century* (Groningen: Groninger Museum, Bai Publishers, 1997)

Anna Wintour, *The South Bank Show* (1997) [quoted on page 172]

Yohji Yamamoto, "The Past, the Feminine, the Vain", in *Talking to Myself* (Göttingen: Steidl/ Edition 7L, 2002)

INDEX

First and foremost I would like to thank my husband Paul for his encouragement and patience whilst I toiled over writing this book. Thanks also to Kate Osborn (my right hand), to Lucy Bishop who helped take many of the beautiful photographs, and Anoushka der Sarkissian who helped proof read.

Hugh Devlin and Sarah Polden have been stalwart supporters and friends throughout and I am forever grateful for their kindness, help, and advice. Murray Blewett, Steven Philip, Hubert de Givenchy, Sally Tuffin, Zandra Rhodes, Stevie Stewart, and Christopher Kane have all given freely of their knowledge, opinions, and memories.

My friend and fellow auctioneer Leslie Hindman supplied the superb American couture images. Jorge Jarur Bascunan allowed me to dip into his fabulous collection for missing pieces and Harold Koda allowed access to the Metropolitan Museum archive – without which this book would be incomplete.

ACKNOWLEDGMENTS

A FIREFLY BOOK

Published by Firefly Books Ltd. 2013

First printing

Publisher Cataloging-in-Publication Data (U.S.)

A CIP record for this title is available from the Library of Congress

Library and Archives Canada Cataloguing in Publication

A CIP record for this title is available from Library and Archives Canada

Published in the United States by
Firefly Books (U.S.) Inc.
P.O. Box 1338, Ellicott Station
Buffalo, New York 14205

Published in Canada by
Firefly Books Ltd.
50 Staples Avenue, Unit 1
Richmond Hill, Ontario L4B 0A7

Printed in China

This title was developed by Mitchell Beazley,
an imprint of Octopus Publishing Group Ltd,
Endeavour House, 189 Shaftesbury Avenue,
London, WC2H 8JY

For Mitchell Beazley:
Publisher Alison Starling; **Editor** Pauline Bache; **Copy Editor** Robert Anderson;
Art Director Jonathan Christie; **Design** Untitled; **Picture Research Manager**
Giulia Hetherington; **Picture Research** Claire Gouldstone; **Production**
Controller Sarah Kramer;